PERSPECTIVE

Other Books by Lee Thayer

PERSPECTIVE

How Our Lives Get Channeled

LEE THAYER

To order additional copies of this book, contact:
Xlibris
1-888-795-4274
www.Xlibris.com
Orders@Xlibris.com
764456

CONTENTS

Perspective 1

A Perspective on Perspective

Every human mind is created – and subsequently maintained or altered – in some form of human communication. The "stuff" of the mind is *meaning* – what things mean to you because that's what things generally mean to those around you, as nearly as you can determine from observing and inquiring. What's at play in the most ordinary everyday conversation all the way to the symbolic posturing of nation-states or bands of true believers of one stripe or another are the minds (and thus the meanings) that the people involved bring to bear.

No two minds are exactly alike. The less contact there is with other minds that may be different from yours, the more convergence there is in the group you belong to. The more contact there is, the more divergences emerge, sometimes violently. Human groups speciate by the social protocols they invent for discerning who belongs to their group from those who do not. Every community is an *epistemic community* – those who belong to them know roughly the same things, and they employ similar ways of arriving at the knowledge they share. This is as much the case for scientists as it is for garbage collectors. They both have an argot, a way of taking about things that is intended to differentiate them from other epistemic communities. Accountants talk and think like accountants, and physical therapists talk and think like physical therapists. Rich people talk and think like rich people, and Marines talk and think like Marines. Chefs talk and think like chefs, and rock music fans talk and think like rock music fans. Amateur gardeners talk and think like amateur gardeners. Etc.

+++++

It is not exactly myopia, depending upon how central and exclusive these orientations are to the lives of the people involved. They are simply ubiquitous perspectives that make our minds more or less unique. People who immigrate to America have a very different perspective on America than those who were born here. People whose native language is unrelated to English have a different perspective than do those of us whose only language is English. People who struggle and achieve virtuosity in any field of endeavor have a very different perspective on life than those who are content with the mediocrity of their lives. Those who survive a near-fatal illness or injury have a different perspective on their lives, and often on the world. And those who have lived lives where nothing much has ever happened have a different perspective on life than do those to whom much has happened. Helen Keller's perspective on the world she came to know only later in her life was significantly different from those whose began life with their eyesight and hearing intact. The surgeon's perspective is different from the farmer's perspective, while the perspective of both is different from that of the airline pilot and the miner.

When people shared the same world as their clan or their neighbors, their perspective – the place from which they viewed the world in their mind's eye – was very similar. A community was a place where people thought very much alike, felt very much alike, and behaved very much alike. There are still remnants in many Amish communities. A special child in such communities might grow up wondering if there is a world out there which might be very different from his or her own. They are free to go find out. If they want to return, it may be under quarantine. They can't be admitted back as a member of the community in good standing unless they abide by its collective beliefs and practices.

They have to be vetted as if they were aliens seeking admission to the community.

There was a time not so long ago when every human who arrived on earth was brought up in such communities. We belonged to them. As those communities have disappeared in the onslaught of modernization, so has the perspective we once had of belonging to one. We moderns are more likely to belong to an occupational group, to some sort of organization, or to those with whom we share leisure-time activities. As communities of people have disappeared, we have lost some or all of our sense of belonging. We moderns belong more often to anonymous groups – such as those we experience vicariously when we watch television, or when we attend a ball game or a pop music concert. We are there, *where it's at*. But there is no there, there. In a few hours, it is over. We may gather with our buddies at a bar to watch the game and imbibe, but all of that ends when the game is over, except for our desperate replays, when we try to keep the camaraderie going so we can belong to *something*. The belonging felt by forming into *us* and *them* categories fades in modernity to something more like *me* and *them* – the "them" being the rest of the world that has no more than marketing interest in "my" existence. The me becomes an anonymous part of some kind of demographic, which younger people try desperately to distinguish themselves in. There is no community to socialize them, beyond a local gang or a larger cause like ISIS. We belong to a category of consumers, within which we struggle for status by how we talk or what we wear or where we hang out.

When we talk we represent the perspective of some ideology or other. We would speak for ourselves. But we are less and less certain of who that is. The rise of me-ism coincides with the decline of community. In a community, we know who we are. In the modern world, who we *are* is always negotiable depending upon who we are talking to. We fit our perspectives to adapt to those we happen to be with.

+++++

Because we are humans, we have to see ourselves and our worlds from *some* perspective. It is impossible to be cognizant of our worlds or ourselves except from our own perspective. Nor is it possible to be routinely cognizant of the world from others' perspectives. It is part of the human condition. The perspective we use to comprehend the world and ourselves in it is socially constructed and maintained. It is what we stand on to conceive of and "understand" the world we inhabit. Without a perspective, we would have no mind. Our perspective, immediate and long-term, comes from how we *mind* the world and ourselves in it.

Mind is a noun. We should think of it as a verb. It is not a place. It is a process. It is the process that determines what we see and how we see it – in terms of the meaning it has for us. The mind is what converts the raw data of the world inside or outside of us into what it means to us. It is the process that determines not only what we "see" in our world, but how we see it. It is as well what we use to process how we present ourselves in our worlds – not only what we say or how we comport ourselves, but how we explain those worlds and ourselves in it. We do this more by what we do than by what we say. Just as we are incessantly "reading" other people and the circumstances, they are incessantly reading us and the circumstances that provoke our attention. This is what minds are for. It is useful to think of this as minding the world.

We don't mind the world according to what it is. We don't perceive the world as *it* is. We perceive the world and perform ourselves in it according to the way *we* are. It is not the way the world *is* but the ways in which we explain it that drives our psychological and social machinations. Our destiny – both personal and collective – lies in how we explain things. We explain things according to our personal and cultural perspectives. We are not obligated to perceive the way the world is, but we are destined to perceive the world according to how we and our cohorts explain it.

Our perspectives trickle down to us from our predecessors (who train us not in the world's ways, but in their ways). We stand on those perspectives to formulate our own interpreted experiences in life. This conglomeration, always in process, may be good for the individual or good for the collective. It may also be deleterious for the individual – *and* for the collective. The mind is not beholden to any "truth" beyond human truths. Of the making of those, there is apparently no end. There are no facts that any mind is obligated to defer to. Minds defer to other minds, not to any facts.

How we have come to see the world (and ourselves in it) determines how we will see the world. The world does not determine how we perceive it. Our perspectives do. We are far more likely to perceive the world the way our social cohorts do than to perceive it as it "is." We can't know the world as it is. We can only know it according to how our collective/individual minds work. We have no choice but to interpret the world according to the interpretations available to us in our own minds. Our perspectives may be similar to those we cohort with. But the perspectives of other cultures alien to ours are perspectives we do not have because we are not one of *them*.

If you are not thoroughly immersed in *their* ways of explaining things, and the vocabulary in which they do so, you cannot grasp fully what they mean by what they say…or do. A perspective on the world which is not habitual and inescapable is not a perspective. It is an anomaly. If you are not a regular golfer, you will not fully understand what regular golfers are talking about when they talk about the game. If you are a Shakespeare or a Packers fan, others who do not share your perspective will be incapable of any real understanding of what that means to you. If you are "in love," a person who has not been in love has no way of seeing the world as you do when you talk about it. Talk is not so much about what you are purportedly talking about as it is about the social relationships in which you are talking. The first and vital function of talking is mental copulation – of trying to be of the same mind about things. It never fully comes about. *People cannot share the "same" perspective. They can only share talk about it.* This may lead them closer to you, or away from you. You may like the people who seem to be coming from the same place you are. But because they cannot, and you cannot, we have to pretend we are (to use a popular cliché) "on the same page." The same page does not and cannot, of course, exist. It's just a metaphor used socially to facilitate moving on. We want to think and feel like others in our purview do. That's because we are (or want to be) related to them in some way. We will never be of exactly the same mind about anything. A mind is not a commodity to be filled or emptied at will. It is the cumulative process that underwrites every individual life. There are no two individual lives that are identical. People inevitably harbor different perspectives about what they presume to be the same things.

A perspective is what we stand on in order to interpret the world. You are not free to see the world in any way you might want to. What you are capable of seeing – or how you feel about it or comprehend it – is a function of who *you* are. What you are incapable of seeing – or how – is also a function of who you are. People see the world from their own private perspective (no matter how influenced by their culture or the subcultures they belong to). What complicates the process is that it is an amalgam of three levels of perspective: (1) That of the larger culture into which they have been thoroughly or haphazardly socialized; (2) That of the epistemic communities* they belong to on purpose or by default; and (3) That of their own experiences and how they have more or less creatively interpreted and explained those experiences to themselves.

*(An epistemic community is a set of people who have more or less similar perspectives on things. They more or less know the same things, and they more or less use the same kind of perspectives for knowing.)

Like most mammals, humans have an inherent need to belong. Belonging is a form of social control. When an individual is rejected or fails to fulfill the reciprocal imperatives of belonging to a group of some sort, he or she becomes a kind of free radical in society – belonging only to an epistemic community of one. They become idiosyncratic, taking their clues about thought and behavior from themselves. They become not just disjunctive, but minimally a threat to the social order. Some become a threat to themselves. A few become a threat to others. This was rarer in traditional communities, because they did a better job of socializing their young. In modern societies, this becomes more prevalent. The combination of poor socialization added to the pull of fashion and of alienation (from any belonging-to) is a breeding ground for both sociopaths and psychopaths. To belong is to belong to the fate of the whole. Not to belong is a failure to have a perspective on life that puts the life of the group first and oneself second. Their self-made perspectives are often toxic to others whose perspectives come from the subcultures to which they have a vital sense of belonging. Self-control comes from the imperatives of belonging. People who don't have those perspectives are led into the dark areas outside of self-control. They become the judge and jury of their own feelings and actions.

Such failures to belong, along with the reciprocal obligations of belonging, seem to lead people to life without a *conscience*. One's conscience is an internalization of the norms and values of the group(s) one belongs to. With it comes all sorts of prescriptions and proscriptions about how to comport oneself in life. The less sense of belonging one has, the more impoverished his or her conscience. It isn't that they don't have a conscience. It is that their conscience is constructed from their personal perspectives, not those of the social groups they do not belong to. They seek to belong to a group that seems to share their personal perspectives. It is the norms and values of *that* group they want to align with. If belonging to that group helps them to shuck off the beliefs and values of the group they want to escape from, so much the better. There is always a group for pariahs to belong to. If there isn't, they will invent one. A person who doesn't want to be like her parents will find comrades who will induct her into a group having that perspective. There are very few hermits in the world. That requires some competencies most people don't have – such as a tolerance for solitude, which most believe to be loneliness.

+++++

It is perspective that creates our differences. It is likewise perspective that creates our similarities. When we have what John Gardner referred to as "Common Cause," we come together. Lacking that, we dissimulate. We assume that it is better to be a hypocrite than not to be a member in good standing of some social or religious or occupational group. Prospective employees often "fib" to become a member of any organization that will have them – and pay them. People who want something from other people will readily deceive them about their intentions. Some people who wanted no more than a one night stand end up with a commitment for life. Some people who wanted a lifetime commitment got no more than a one night stand. A car salesperson or a diamond ring salesperson might sell you what you don't need. That's because it is about what *they* need, not what you need.

In our culture, there are always people out there who are *Phishing for Phools*, as Akerlof and Shiller entitled their book about the economics of manipulation and deception. If people want something badly enough, they are likely to forget the principle of *caveat emptor* (let the buyer beware). By and large, we do not equip our children with adequate immunity to such manipulations and deceptions as are practiced daily. That may be because parents and teachers and friends are themselves likely practitioners of manipulation and deception. Most people wouldn't even know how to seek advice that might be good for them. We are not open to advice that might require any significant changes in the ruts we are making on a daily basis with our lifestyles. How we perform our lives may not be good for us. But they are normative. And we would much rather be good consumers than good people – if that is what is required to belong. First we import our perspectives from people or groups we are compelled to – or desire to – belong to. And then those perspectives create us. They are our master habits. We live by them. Most people seem content to die by them. Why? *Simply because that is their perspective on things.*

+++++

It is impossible to comprehend the world – or to comprehend oneself in it – except from some perspective. For example:

- We start conscious (self-reflexive) life in the context of those who nurture us in infancy. The change from non-language existence and language usage in society (as Helen Keller so eloquently expressed) may be the most radical change of perspective in all of our lives. We begin to comprehend the world (and us in it) from the perspective of those who guide us in this second birth – into how we explain the world linguistically and behaviorally.

- Perhaps the next most dramatic (though tacit and gradual) change in perspective occurs as we age. The longer you live, the more past you assume you have. The longer you live, the less future you assume you have. Over the years, you cease learning how to comprehend the world and begin comprehending the world according to the familiar (from repeated use) perspectives that have become embedded in the way you "see" the world (and yourself in it). The mind, as plastic as it is, ossifies. We don't grow mentally. We plateau. As a result, at some point in our lives we begin the slippery slope of cognitive degeneration. The mind flourishes only when it is growing. When it is not growing, it degenerates.

- From infancy, the next most notable change in perspective comes when we begin to relate to peers of a similar age. If we like them, we begin to entertain the possibilities of comprehending the world from their point of view. A friendship is a willingness to experiment with seeing the world as the other person sees it. A failed friendship is a failure to do so. We create common ground in sharing our perspectives on the world (and us in it). We create shared realities by explaining them to each other. When actual friends won't do, we create imaginary friends who will. We begin to see ourselves as others see us. This is often such a frightening perspective that most people guard against it the rest of their lives. We grow up (sometimes) in the maelstrom of differing perspectives on who we are.

- At some point in our early lives, another radically different perspective begins to dawn on us. There are really two kinds of people in our worlds. One kind is physically like us. The other kind is physically different from us. Boys and girls are different. They even have different perspectives on the actual world we sometimes have to share. What to make of this, and what to do about this, becomes a major project of puberty. At the outset of the realization, the other gender is alien. The accommodations we make are largely serendipitous. They simply occur. We're curious about these different creatures. They look different. They smell different. Their voices come at us in a different range. It is like learning a foreign language. One is hairy. The other is not. It isn't until later that you learn why this is so. In puberty, you don't yearn to rocket into space. You already are.

• Somewhere along the time that you discover that there are two very different kinds of human creatures, you are also introduced to the mass media and to your electronically-connected worlds. When not distracted by the special effects of movies or television, you begin to perceive that there is not only a "natural" world you do not control (or comprehend), but that there is a human-made technological world that brings you entertainment and games of every sort (whose instigation and delivery mechanisms you are also not privy to). We learn to comprehend our worlds more superficially, more literally, and more consumptively. We become indentured to the fashions of the day – what feeling are in or out, what beliefs are in or out, what ways of comporting oneself in public are in or out, etc. As we are developing minds of our own, we begin to see that our minds are not "our own," but are manipulated by others, especially our personal celebrities and those that we otherwise trust. We learn to deceive…and to be deceived. In a "free world," we are as likely to be a victim as we are to victimize others.

• As part of the epiphanies we have growing up, we begin to realize (if we have had competent parents, teachers, and friends) that perspective is a function of the cultures and subcultures that people belong to. Or have belonged to: Those who preceded us in our society had different perspectives than we do on life and the worlds in which they had them. That doesn't make either set of perspectives right or wrong. Just different. The critical issue is… where do your perspectives lead you? Are they efficacious for you and those around you? Are they efficacious for the destiny of your society? If not, shouldn't they be?

- We acquire the perspectives we stand on to comprehend our worlds and ourselves in them. It is never obvious to us – any more than our breathing is – how vital and influential is the matter of who we hang out with, who or what we have mental intercourse with. Friends influence the way we think. Good friends influence us more. What we read influences the way our minds work. If you read junk, your mind will turn to junk. Commercial advertisers are influential. They provide us with short stories that we may try to live out ourselves. The premises of the games we play – electronic or social – can easily become our premises, our perspectives, on our lives. In school, "A" students are inclined to hang out with "A" students, "D" students with "D" students. If you think learning is a dumb activity, you will tend to hang out with peers who feel the same way. By their jokes and other innuendos, you will be infused.

- When people speak to you, directly or electronically, they are speaking from their perspective. If you consume "the news," you will come to see the world that way. There is no news which is not highly selective. Commercially, the news that gets distributed is based on the size of the audience and its purchasing power. Socially, the news that gets distributed brings status. The more central one's status in any social group or social circle, the more influential one is. What people tell us (that we are susceptible to), the more likely we are to repeat it, and the more likely it fits our personal perspectives on the world (and us in it). Speaking is potentially contagious, whether to ourselves or to others.

- As listeners or viewers, we bring our perspectives to bear on what we see and hear. If it is confirmatory (of the way we already see the world), we like it. If it is not, we are unlikely to attend to it. The mind works on ROA – Return on Attention. It tries to attend to what will give us the most pleasure or confirmation. When possible, it ignores perspectives that are disconfirming or discombobulating. We see our worlds not from the world's perspective, but from ours. The world we know – and how we know it – are a function of our perspectives, not a function of the way the world *is*.

- Scientist or chimney sweep, our perspectives serve up the world to us. We don't seek to gain more efficacious perspectives. We seek out people who will confirm the ones we already have – for good or ill.

- Stories (or works of art or of currently popular music) are meaningful if they suit the perspectives we take to them. People don't see or hear what is there. They see or hear what their perspectives enable them to see or hear. All the rest they dismiss out of hand. We like what we like. We dislike what we dislike. We attribute our likings to what we see. But what we see or hear is a function of us, not of what we are looking at or listening to. Our personal perspectives determine *how* we see what we see or how we hear what we hear. They enable certain worlds and meanings. They disable others. You cannot see or hear the world objectively. It cannot be done without a subjective perspective. And that perspective is at least a bias, if not a prejudice. An ideology is a basic perspective. It is like wearing armor. It enables certain conclusions, but prevents others.

- If you change where you live on this earth, your perspectives will change. If you move to a different house, your perspectives will change. If you change partners for any reason, your perspectives will change. If you change your work place or if you change your work role, your perspectives will change. If for any reason, you change your lifestyle, your perspectives will change. If you change your way of dress, your perspectives will change. If you are told you might die of your disease, your perspectives change. If you cease to depend on the faiths you once held sacred, your perspectives will change. If you are a virgin, you will have a certain perspective on things. When you are no longer a virgin, your perspectives change. When you strongly desire something, you will have a certain perspective on life. When you obtain what you desired, your perspective changes. When you have hopes or even concrete plans for the future, and they do not come about, your perspective changes. When you knew what was true, you had a certain perspective. When that turns out not to be tenable, your perspectives change. When your life's story changes (for any reason), your perspectives on life will change. Feeling lucky or unlucky are two very different perspectives on life. Falling in love changes your perspective on things. Being dumped changes your perspective on love. Perspectives are averse to contrary perspectives. What happens is not a happening as such. It is your perspective on the happening that matters.

+++++

We may think we are in charge of our feelings, our thinking, and our doing. There's nothing wrong with this little bit of self-deception. Or is there? Sometimes people make bad decisions or bad judgments. Sometimes people make poor choices. And many times they blame themselves for being so stupid. Then the self-deception becomes harmful. It may not be them, as such. It may be that the perspectives they brought to the situation or imposed upon the situation were not the ones they needed. Once they are operative and thus tacit, we do not control our perspectives. It is our perspectives that control or channel us. We accumulate our perspectives over time and from myriad sources. In the culture and subcultures we belong to, they are invasive. We have little awareness of their painless organization of our minds. We assume they are simply part of who we are. They become not only the guiding mechanisms of who we are. We become who we are as a result of the perspectives we exercise. They are the premises by which we live. Once established, they are subtle but insidious. We live by them.

But we are rarely aware of living by them. They are not only the answer to our prayers. They are the source of our prayers – of our hopes, our dreams, and our expectations. The meanings we impose upon our world come from our perspectives on that world. We are in-formed by them. The information and entertainment we import is in their service, not ours.

+++++

Our perspectives on the world and us in it are vital. They are also problematical. We pretend that they are givens, rarely realizing that they are social artifacts, with all of the vagaries of social artifacts. If we were to change the sources of our perspectives, we would be – both individually and collectively – different than we are. Perhaps even better.

The balance of this book is given over to exploring the sources and the consequences of the perspectives we happen to live by. We cannot know the ultimate "truth" of things. We can only have our perspectives on what we then assume is reality. More often than not, our realities are socially constructed. The more we understand about where they come from and where they lead, the better our choices – and thus our lives – could be.

Perspective 2

Sources and Consequences

Everything that is comprehended has to be seen from *some* perspective. How we see the eagle is not how the eagle sees us. How we see a baby is not how the baby sees us. How we see other people is not the way those other people see us. Influential painters and photographers have certainly changed the way we see the world we live in. Folk artists have been doing so for millennia. Writers and filmmakers have changed the way we think about and apprehend our lives – and imagine other worlds – past and future. Some artists, like Michelangelo, and some writers, like Cervantes, have created ways of seeing and thinking about the *ideal* human and the *ideal* life. Other artists and writers have depicted the opposite of the ideal – and everything in between and beyond.

But the major changes in perspective in recent times came from the invention of the mirror and the camera. They enabled us to see ourselves as others saw us and have forever changed our relationships and our societies. At one time past, and for millennia, we had to depend upon others to prepare us for going out in public. With a mirror, we can do that for ourselves.

The myth was that Narcissus saw his reflection in a pool of water. And he fell in love with…his reflection. These days people can do that anytime of the day or night using the camera in their smart phones, if their arms are long enough, and if they are hungry enough to see one more reflection of themselves. The myth of the "self," just emerging in Narcissus' time, is at the core of our modern beliefs about who we "are."

The mirror is pivotal in human civilization and in how we comprehend ourselves and our worlds. The idea of individualism – and thus even of democracy – was essentially unthinkable before the mirror, which provided us with what we took to be objective evidence of our otherwise wholly subjective sense of ourselves. In modern society, we are poseurs. We posture and comport ourselves as if we were being seen by the camera. Such changes as these wrought were not incremental. They were epochal, as epochal as the invention of gunpowder. They have changed the course of human civilization and of our lives therein.

+++++

Ideas are at the same time explanations. They explain the lives we have had, the lives we could have, and how we are supposed to see ourselves and our worlds. They create the perspectives we have for interpreting our worlds and the conditions of our lives within them. Explanations are the primordial and the contemporary artifacts of human life. They enable us to make sense of our circumstances – past, present, and future. That we see our (Western) world in terms of the present, the past, and the future is the prime exemplar of how ideas have consequences. Ideas make possible other ideas, make contradictory ideas less possible. They can be translated into other related ideas or they can be translated into some aspect of our material worlds. The mirror was once an idea. That idea made tangible was the mirror. Various forms of preventing conception came from the idea that conception could be (and thus *should* be) controlled by choice. A path used by animals became a path used by humans. Those became roads and the roads became highways. Those highways became highways in the sky. Where ideas and their applications are concerned, one thing leads to another. The idea of where we *should* be going from our perspective, antiquated) gets lost in the onrush of where our ideas and their manifestations are taking us. Neither ideas nor their manifestations have a conscience. Our perspective is what we can do with our technologies, not where they are leading us. We make things in the image of our talk about them. And then they make us.

The mind is a human/socially-made virtual device for creating ideas and for comprehending oneself and one's worlds – a meaning-making, meaning-subscribing kind of device. The worlds we inhabit are increasingly less "natural" and increasingly more virtual. For the most part, our virtual worlds are more real to us than is any real world. The world may or may not be filled with data (since "data" is a concept invented by people). But we deal with our worlds only in terms of what we have made them *mean* to us. What surpasses the meanings we have for things surpasses our ability to comprehend it. Our perspective on things is some indecipherable congeries of the meanings we have available to relate ourselves to them, and those things we comprehend to one another. It has repeatedly been observed: We do not see the world as it "is." We must necessarily see the world as *we* are – as our perspectives on things enable us to see and disable us from seeing. As Emerson put it: *"What we are, that only can we see."* The natural world and the social worlds we inhabit are a function of our perspectives – what they *mean* to those of us who belong." We plan and execute our lives according to what things happen to mean to us. In a traditional social world (one far more homogeneous than our modern worlds) people attributed more or less the same meanings to themselves and the circumstances of their mutually-conceived of world. In our "modern" worlds, we balkanize our societies. We think of them as open to new and different perspectives, as ever-evolving, and the new perspectives as rendering obsolete the old perspectives. Ours is a world of ever-emerging subcultures, fashions, and of obsolescence. We don't have one in-common perspective. We have as many differing perspectives as are made possible by the epistemic communities that people can invent or want to belong to. In our cities, for example, we may not even know the names of our neighbors – or care much one way of the other about them. The occupational or other epistemic communities may be far-flung, across the country or around the world. Theoretical physicists talk to theoretical physicists and share their perspectives on things. Artists talk to artists and plumbers talk to plumbers. Professors talk to professors and students talk to students.

People who imagine they are smart prefer talking to people who imagine they are smart. People who have no particular aspirations in life prefer to hang out with people who share their perspectives on the world. Protestantism was invented as an alternative to Catholicism. But today there are many forms of Protestantism. But the Amish may not want to mix it up with the Episcopalians.

To *belong* is to share the perspectives of the others who belong to this or that social group. One belongs if one shares that group's ways of knowing, being, and doing. You know what you are expected to know. You are who you are expected to be. And you perform your life more or less as you are expected to perform your life. Perspectives are like core beliefs. They underwrite what you are supposed to know and think and feel, and what you are supposed to do – and how you are supposed to do what you do.

+++++

Most conflicts in life originate in conflicts of perspective. It is a conflict of discordant perspectives that manifests itself in marital discord. Most wars are fought over differing perspectives. Pugilists have differing (and hidden) perspectives when the fight is on. So do competing poker players. The courtiers of courted kings and queens often had differing perspectives than did those kings and queens, who historically were most often deposed by their trusted courtiers. This happens about half the time in modern marriages.

Our personal identities emerge from the epistemic communities to which we initially belong. If we lose our belongingness, our perspective on ourselves is in jeopardy. Pariahs are not necessarily dangerous. But they suffer the consequences of no longer being a member-in-good-standing in any social group. Social groups are a way of social control and socialization. Without belonging, pariahs become like free radicals, whether benign or toxic to others or to society. This is common in our modern worlds.

When people feel that they share a destiny in common, they will share a compatible set of perspectives on the essential aspects of their lives. When righteous people were assumed to ascend to heaven, it made sense of "love they neighbor," because you could be sharing the same bench there. The social arrangements will not be as they were on earth – or before reincarnation. If there is to be harmony, the short-term or long-term objectives of relating at all will most likely be commonly held perspectives. We bring a set of perspectives to any relationship – else they may have to emerge from the relationship itself. Either way, compatible perspectives will determine the nature of the relationship. It is a stereotype, of course, but if he is addicted to football on TV and she doesn't like it at all, they will be at odds at least as long as the game is on. The less those basic perspectives are shared, the more precarious is the relationship. Trouble is always brewing in the modern world. What's at stake is whose perspectives are to dominate which relationships.

What's at stake in marriages is the marriage. What's at stake in friendships is the contribution to personal identity of the friendship. What's at stake in civil uprisings or rebellions is the destiny of the larger society. What's at stake when gangs or sects conflict is hegemony – whose perspectives can be made to dominate the other? Dogs are "owned" by those in the household. They had no say in where they ended up. If in France, they learn to respond to French language commands. If in Russia, Russian. If in Brazil, Portuguese. It's the same with human babies. They don't chose who to have as their parents. But as adults we can choose who or what to be influenced by. Those choices, built atop the earlier influences which we did not choose, will determine what our perspectives and thus our lives will be like. About our lives to date, we may have no choice. But about our future lives we do. We are not born with the perspectives that channel our lives. Those we get from the people we hang out with – directly or indirectly (reading, for example), living or dead. Incrementally and cumulatively, as we choose the makers of our perspectives, we choose the paths of our lives.

+++++

Incrementally and cumulatively for two reasons:

1. We are not born with a mind of our own. Minds are not a biological product. They are socially created. They normally arise in being talk to, read to, and from naming things. If born in France, to French-speaking people, we are highly likely to see the world as they do. Our ways of seeing the world (and us in it) will almost certainly derive from the episteme of the people we learn to converse with and the indigenous media they expose us to. No matter how thoughtlessly or strategically done, that will provide the foundation for any further development of our individual minds. Our minds evolve incrementally from the foundations laid there – for better or for worse. The more different the opportunities for the development of one's mind, the richer and more complex it will be. That is why the enlightened royalty and upper classes of the past devoted as much time to the development of their offspring's minds as they did to the development of their bodies and their social skills. There are always risks. You may have to forfeit existing and familiar relationships in order to gain ones that may propel you to a more efficacious life and destiny. Social groups perpetuate themselves. They have no concern for where they are leading their members. You cannot be who you wish to be without giving up who you presently are. You have to barter who you are for who you hope to be. Largely as a consequence of how we put to use the mirror and the camera in our everyday lives, we place more value on our short-term personas in our social circles than we do on our long-term destinies.

    Consider well: People do not intend to impair their future lives by becoming mentally obese. That is some observer's perspective. They are merely exercising their *right* to consume mentally (and physically) what they "like." They don't read serious literature because it is "hard" – or because it is not what they have a pop-culture appetite for. *You can no more have a healthy body by consuming nutrition-starved food than you can have a healthy mind by consuming stuff for the mind that is without nutrition for the mind.*

That is likely to be someone else's perspective. It is that one perspective is not per se better than the other. It is that the perspectives you bring to bear have *consequences*. Perspectives differ ultimately and pragmatically only in their *consequences* for your present and future life. You came by your perspectives incrementally. You have to change them when they need to be changed in the same way you got them in the first place.

2. The most appropriate term for all of that may be *teleology:* which is intended to imply that all things (including people) grow into what they become out of what they are at any point in time. The perspectives you have determine the kind of perspectives you can have. You can never go back and start over. We are always stuck with being who we have become – *cumulatively*. People often forget this. We are each who we have become, compounded cumulatively. You can only become who you might be out of who you already are. Your perspectives are part of who you are. Changing them changes you, and changing you changes them.

    We are inclined (in our peculiar culture) to believe that there is such a thing as objective "knowledge." This cannot be so. Any "fact" or "truth" or "reality" *that we can talk about* is a human fact or truth or reality. How we explain things is our human reality, not how things may actually be. If they can be talked about, they are human truths, the only kind we can talk about. Any human communication, no matter the subject, begins in an interpretation and ends in an interpretation. Our interpretations are channeled by what things mean to us. And these may vary from person to person, and from time to time. Your spouse may have loved you yesterday, but may not "feel" that way today.

Our basic perspectives may have the staying power of habits. But our satellite perspectives come and go as does the weather. Minds cannot be empirically mapped or understood. They are dynamic, not fixed. They may make the world go 'round, but we cannot ultimately understand them in all of their dynamic complexity. That's because we have to understand them from the only perspective we have for doing so – our own minds. They change and grow (or not) cumulatively. They quickly grow cumulatively beyond our ken. They have a mind of their own, which is largely beyond our control.

+++++

A perspective is the cumulative ground we stand on to look at ourselves and our worlds. Joyce Carol Oates makes a rather challenging observation as an author's note in *Them* (1969):

> *"This is a work of history in fictional form – that is, in personal perspective, which is the only kind of history that exists."*

What she's intimating is that there is no history written from any but a personal perspective – personal or collective. We all have a vague sense of our own personal histories, which are typically a mixed bag of remembered details (reconstructed in hindsight). We are the ones who weave them into a kind of plausible story (usually based on existing public stories) that we tell ourselves, and then tell others.

There are invariably two kinds of perspectives:

1. There are perspectives that are unique to every individual. That's because there are no two individuals alike in the way they experience and interpret their worlds.

2. Then there are "generic" perspectives – cultural perspectives that are shared by large numbers of people. They are popular perspectives imbibed by people in their cultures as if by osmosis.

So the perspectives that people exercise in their everyday lives are always some combination of their cultural orientations and their personal experiences. How any person sees the world (and themselves in it) will be based in cultural perspectives, but always tempered by their immediate, personal outlook on things.

So the histories that Oates writes about may derive from currently-fashionable cultural formulas for writing histories, just as there are currently fashionable formulas for taking photographs. But they will always bear the imprint of the person who talked about or wrote about them – the person who made them. Like all of what we like to refer to as reality or truth, personal and collective explanations of our pasts have both cultural underpinnings and personal proclivities in the way they are told. We fictionalize the past so that it seems to be a plausible explanation of the present or the future. We fictionalize the future so that it seems to be an inevitable outcome of our present and our pasts.

What we "see" and how we see it depends on the perspective from which we are seeing it. Having an amorous perspective will lead you to see your potential partner differently than you would otherwise. If you are angry with your world, you will look upon it differently then you would if you were pleased with it. One old saying about this is:

> *"Tell me what you are thinking about all day and*
> *I'll tell you who you are."*

What we think about depends on our perspective on the world (and ourselves). And we become what we think about – and how we do so. Most people these days live in a world that has to be explained to them. They are impaired, and willing to let their thinking be done for them by commercial interests. Few of the people who lived before us were so impaired. They had to learn how to think – or they would die. We moderns don't read or watch television, or gather at sports or celebrity events or watering holes to learn how to think – or even what's worth thinking about. We just want to be able to talk about what others in our social circles will be talking about. Henry Ford observed that thinking is the hardest thing we have to do, and therefore most people have so successfully avoided it that they *can't* think.

The more impoverished one's mind, the more impoverished will be a person's capacity for perceiving the world they live in. The less relevant you feel to the world you inhabit, the less relevant you will feel to yourself. People who don't like the world they inhabit will generally not like themselves. Perspective has a way of being reciprocal.

Why is *that?* To begin to think about that, you have to recognize that you cannot see the world independently of who (or what) you are. People attribute their perspectives on the world they are capable of seeing. They refer to it as "reality." If you don't like the world you live in, it will seem inescapable to you that it doesn't like you. It's the same between two people: if you don't like the other person, that other person will seem not to like you. It is impossible for one person to make a love affair with another person...or a hate affair. The world outside of you mirrors your feelings toward it, much like a mirror does. You will see other people or the circumstances of your life from the perspectives you can invoke.

There was good reason for American Indian tribes to make it a *duty* to the tribe to be happy. That perspective was refracted back by their cohorts and their culture. It was also their *duty* not to be sick. For the Europeans who displaced or annihilated them, sickness was expected. It makes a difference what perspectives are brought to bear in private and public life.

It is the same in every communication encounter with another person or the media. The original term for "communication" was "intercourse" – making it abundantly clear that every such encounter involved human minds and therefore carried the risk of consequences. Minds "copulate," to borrow the metaphor offered by the longshoreman-turned-social philosopher Eric Hoffer. When they copulate in every communication encounter, they create the virtual worlds which are the inevitable consequences of their copulation. That is the source of the meaning of things – to those of us who share the consequences. The stuff of the mind is essentially meanings. It is not *the* world that we inhabit, but *a* world of our own creation. The source of perspective is human explanation. And the consequences are that the perspectives we impose on the world become that world that we consciously inhabit. We derive our identities in that virtual world. In communication, you are either influencing or being influenced. We are created as persons in those encounters. And we maintain who we think we are by choosing those encounters that we take to confirm who we are, and shun those that would bring that illusion into jeopardy. If people have no overriding cause or purpose in life, then they are just along for wherever others' influences take them.

Bona fide hermits don't change much during their hermitage. Neither would you if you never fell into a conversation with others. The more removed people are from their society, the easier it is for them to create or cling to idiosyncratic perspectives. We see this in teenage suicides and in cognitive degeneration as people age. Traditional societies were relatively "closed." In a permissive and more "open" society, one changes with the *fashions* in beliefs, in feelings, and in ever-changing recipes for living.

+++++

To recap and rephrase:

- In a modern, open, and permissive society like our own, the monolithic culture is being constantly challenged and splintered by the fashions of the day. The fashions of the day arise and are displaced in the smaller subcultures people belong to. Most of those alive today grew up and were socialized into one or more of these popular cultures. Such subcultures, which we choose or are seduced into, function like the air we breathe. We pay it no heed unless something goes wrong and we have to. Who we "are" is always at risk in such circumstances. If we don't keep up to date in our thoughts and our beliefs and our comportment, we could become obsolete and lose the security we imagined we had. In such societies, fashion is not trivial. It becomes central to who we are and why.

- An inescapable source of our perspectives on ourselves and our worlds is the people involved in our early upbringing – influences that may have trickled down for several generations. In the modern world, even parents may have diverse opinions about how to best socialize their offspring, how to provide them with the perspectives they will need. In today's world, many children are banished to be socialized by the television and by the other electronic gadgets they are provided with. Increasingly, parents abdicate their responsibility for the lives of their children by turning it over to teachers (maybe as early as two) and to the commercials and commercial programming on television. There are exceptions, but what they are exposed to there is exploitation. Learning how to be exploited and to exploit others is not particularly character-building.

- Most children meet other children earlier than ever before. They become your peers. Most sex education begins in modernity in the schoolyard at about the age of three. That's a pop culture perspective. It is not a considered strategy for mental or emotional hygiene. Children compete to be fashionable – in thought and feeling as well as dress and comportment. In a permissive society popularity rules. Being popular is perhaps not the best platform for a better life as a young adult. It is a perspective – a way of looking at the world and oneself. But it may not be the most efficacious one. Winning a popularity contest is perhaps not what it takes to win at life.

- Then there is the source of perspective that comes from who we hang out with as preteens through adulthood. It would be rare in our time for young adults to go to the trouble of vetting those people in terms of their long-term contribution to their lives. We belong to cliques and social circles not because they will parent us better than did our parents (or than we can), but because they will have us. We do not marry the person who will lead us into a better life, but the person who will have us. The less compelling one's life purposes are, the more desperately will that person seek to *belong* to any group or gang that will have him or her as a member. The perspective required here is that you will belong mainly to your purposes in life, or you will feel the need to belong to any social clutch that will have you. You can be accepted only if you adopt the perspectives of that group or that organization, formal or not. It is difficult for a Marine to adapt to many civilian perspectives. The perspectives required of them as a Marine makes them ill-suited for a free-wheeling pop culture. To belong to the smaller society ("the" Marines) makes their transition problematic. It is the same for many such transitions. Some sheltered and indulged teenagers can't imagine how they need to change to function in any real world. So they withdraw into a world of their own. People who were married for a length of time may find it difficult to adopt the perspectives required for being single. And vice versa. People who can't read say the writer can't write. That's the way one's perspectives open certain doors in life but close others.

- The most influential person in your life is the one you talk to most often...*you*. After childhood, you are the first person you consult with when you have a problem. You are the last person you talk to when you leave a gathering with others. If you want to know whether or not you are sick, you first consult yourself. If you want to know whether the way you see yourself in your world is the right one, you first consult yourself. If you want to judge another person, the first and the last judgment will be yours. If you want to know whether the world is for you or against you, you will be the final judge and jury, no matter the input of others (solicited or not). If you want to know how you should live your life, advice from diverse perspectives is readily available. It will descend upon you whether you seek it out or not. There are dozens of predators for every human who is troubled or curious.

We all know this of course. Yet the problem is not solved by analyzing it. It is resolved only by the consequences of what you do about it. The rub is this: The perspectives you bring to bear to think about it will largely determine what you will choose to do about it – limited by what you are capable of doing about it. Over the cumulative years of your life, your perspectives will limit what you are capable of doing about your problems or concerns. You can heed good advice, or you can heed bad advice, cumulatively limited by whatever you are capable of doing about your concerns.

> *What you can't imagine yourself doing about life's*
> *twists and turns will be something you* won't *do*
> *about them.*

A person in our supposedly rational world might be inclined to think that people would invariably give themselves good advice – "good" advice being just the advice they need at any juncture of their lives. *If that's the perspective you apply, you would be wrong.*

People can't give themselves any better advice than they are capable of carrying out. We discriminate on the basis of what we are capable of doing about how we see things. And that capability seems to be receding in our modern worlds. And if we don't have the right perspective on things, we can become proficient at doing the wrong things to achieve the lives we might desire. Life without the right kinds of perspectives leads us into quandaries we don't have the perspectives to deal with.

As we move ahead in this book, it will be clearer and clearer to you why this is so – and what you might need to do about it to make your own life go right.

> *Even "Nature is to [people] whatever name*
> *[people] want to give her. We will perceive Nature*
> *according to the names we give her…."*

> Ernest Schachtel, *Metamorphosis*

Perspective 3

Core Perspectives

At the end of the preceding chapter, you were asked to consider how a given culture perceives nature differently. What Schachtel had to say might equally apply to "human" nature. We may attribute more to human nature – as we have come to explain and understand it in our culture – than we do to the *choices* people make over the course of their lives. Our nature will have far more to do with the culture we grew up in than with the assumption that we are all humans on this planet. There are some perspectives that are more like the trunk of a tree and others more like the limbs of a tree (or even the leaves of a tree). There are some perspectives that are more like the roots of a plant. Yet the plants that grow from those roots are all variants on the theme. They are never totally controlled by their roots. It matters how differently they are fertilized, watered, and otherwise tended. Some perspectives are held by a few people, other perspectives by seemingly everyone in your society. Some produce offspring. Others don't. Some are simply more generic and influential than others in the lives we live in our worlds. Some perspectives are core, others are occasional. Some are deeply embedded, others are shallow. Some are broad, others are narrow. Some are fecund. Others may be useful, but barren. Some underlie all or most of our orientations. Others are more superficial, coming or going with our moods.

We perceive our worlds selectively. What attracts our attention is what we have a very low threshold for, what we are expecting to see. What we don't see lies outside of our perspective at the moment, or perhaps permanently. Our core perspectives are those that have become so much a part of us that we take them for granted. They are tacit. We are not consciously aware of them, even though they are channeling our lives. They are a part of our reality, which we rarely, if ever, question. For example, Barbara Kingsolver, in her essay entitled "On Writing, Politics, and Human Nature" (in *The Sun,* March 2014) made this pertinent observation:

> *"...we believe we collect evidence and then use it to make up our minds, but in fact we make up our minds and then collect evidence to support our beliefs...We make these kinds of animal decisions about who's on our team, and then we pretty much believe what they say."*

That's the way perspectives work. We perceive what we expect to perceive, and then we look for the evidence to support our beliefs — which constitute, for the most part, our realities. We subconsciously select who is on "our team" so that we can believe what each other say simply because we belong to the same community of people having pretty much the same perspectives (beliefs) that we do. Using our beliefs (our perspectives) we disambiguate the world looking for what confirms our beliefs and shunning what doesn't. This works well in a monolithic traditional society. But it does not work so well in a society made up of opinion groups of all kinds. We find ourselves in disagreements, which sometimes turn violent. As we have seen, even marital discord can be traced to different perspectives on what we like to imagine is the "same" thing. It isn't the same thing to the two of them. Their differing perspectives make those "same" things different things. Christians disagree. Muslims disagree. And gang members disagree on principle. That's why they shoot each other. If you don't confirm my perspectives, I can settle the argument with a gun or a knife.

How do we "make up our minds"? We could do so idiosyncratically (perhaps), but most minds are ultimately not that autonomous. We are far more likely to make up our minds in a way that is similar to how others in our epistemic communities are likely to make up *their* minds. In other words, when we learn to think and feel like those we socialize with the most, we are likely to synchronize our minds with theirs – and vice versa. We share our opinions with the people we share most of our socializing time with. We "share" because we belong to the same epistemic communities as certain others do. Our perspectives come from our belonging, not from any concern about which perspectives are the most efficacious for those involved, or for the larger society. People in traditional societies thus provide for the destiny of the larger society. People in modern societies have no larger society to belong to, so they think and vote like they do because they belong to the demographic or the splinter groups they belong to.

"Framing" biases our perspectives and hence our interpretations of what others say and do. It is the aim of public relations professionals to frame their messages to seduce more people as customers or as voters or as fans of the celebrity or marketers paying them to do so. But people in everyday life do this as well, so we are used to it. And we do it. We put a "spin" on what we say or do that is intended to cement our relationships with the other people who matter in our lives. We don't say what we mean. We say what is going to improve our status or our relationship with the people we're talking to. You don't say much about your flaws as a human being if you want the other person to fall in love with you. And they do the same. In his *How to Win Friends and Influence People,* Dale Carnegie offers "In a Nutshell – Six Ways to Make People Like You." The sixth one is:

> *"Make the other person feel important – and do*
> *it sincerely."*

It works, of course. He doesn't suggest doing this only if you *are* sincere about doing it. Only if it *seems* sincere to the other person (or persons). In this, he was very modern. We don't live in a world that is candid or honest. We live in a world that functions on appearances and spin. Are you "lying" if you are attempting to make the other person feel important – even if you both know that you are more important than he or she is? Commercial marketers show pictures of what you could look like if you used their cosmetics or wore their clothes and brushed your teeth to brilliant whiteness if you use their toothpaste. Are they sincere? Are they serious? That's not a question in the modern world. The question is: Did it work? Did they "sell" their products or ideas or services by how they made you feel? Are the models and endorsers in those commercials sincere about what they are saying? Or are they good enough actors to make you believe they are sincere? Is the car salesman sincere? Would your pastor put a spin on what he says in order to put more money in the coffers? Would you put a spin on how you talk to your boss at work if you thought it would bring more money in your paycheck? We can surmise that Carnegie is correct, and that his advice about how to make friends and influence people works. But maybe you don't make friends with people just because they are good at making you feel important. What then? What if you use criteria for friendship that are not the conventional ones? What then?

Lord Chesterfield, in a letter to his son in 1750, wrote:

> *"Those whom you can make like themselves will,*
> *I promise you, like you very well."*

In other words, if you can make people like themselves better than they did before you came along, they will like you. In the modern world, as Shakespeare said, we are all actors on a stage – we are always playing a role of some sort in public. If the role you are playing is that of duping those you are playing to, is that somehow immoral or unethical? Or is it just the way society works in the modern world? Would a grocer refuse to sell you products that are inferior? Or is the onus on the customer? Would someone who wanted to lure you into a marriage relationship refuse the tricks that are used to make that happen in order to be "sincere"? What we are seeing here is a core perspective in a culture which is dominated by money, and by status. The fans who stand to applaud their celebrities without knowing whether the music is any good or not are paying money and accolades for what? What are *they* getting out of it? Is poor entertainment better than no entertainment at all? Is this core perspective in modern culture good for you? Is it good for the destiny of your society? We don't stop to think about that because it has by social osmosis become a part of who we are.

Do you like or dislike people who are candid with you? Do you like or dislike people who have the integrity to tell you what they think of you even though that's something you didn't want to hear? In Edward Anthony's *O Rare Don Marquis* (1962), Marquis is quoted as saying:

> *"Some persons are likable in spite of their unswerving integrity."*

But Carnegie is setting forth a perspective for the masses in which integrity is not a criterion to be used. It's probably only those few people of integrity who *like* people of integrity. We tend to like people who are like us. If integrity is not high priority for us, it is not likely to be a high priority criterion for the people we like. Among other functions, the social media permit us to register our likes and dislikes – for the utterances of people we may not know beyond what they posted, and for whom we are for the most part anonymous. Our integrity – or theirs – plays an insignificant role in our opinions. The more "friends" we have, the higher our opinion of ourselves. Friendship becomes a numbers game.

So how important is integrity as a core perspective? You can have friends without it. You can fall in love and get married without it. You can rise to the top in your company without it. You can even be chosen as president of the United States or you can make an unworthy celebrity rich without it. So it seems not to be of importance in our core cultural perspectives. The Marquis of Halifax, in 1750, wrote in his *Reflections*:

> *"A man in a corrupted age must make a secret of his integrity, or else he will be looked upon as a common enemy."*

Writing today, he would of course be referring to a woman as well as to a man, for women too may have such a character, or a lack of it, as is obvious. So he is suggesting that a corrupted age is filled with corrupted people, and that to be known as a person of integrity will likely have the consequence of being seen from the perspective as an irritant to most, if not exactly an enemy of the masses who sees the world from that core perspective. If you are an "average" person, your perspective on the world requires you to be at least suspicious of anyone who appears to have characteristics that you do not champion. (Unless, of course, that more advantaged person socially and economically is one of your favorite celebrities, in which case you forgive them their trespasses if indeed they pander to you as a fan.) People of cultural "merit" have a different perspective on the world (and themselves) than do those who belong to the meritocracy. In India, you are born into a caste, which others have to take heed of in dealings with you. In America, you are born into a privileged caste because of your parents' financial standing, or into a "working" class because you are not affluent, or perhaps even into the welfare class where, as with the others, it is the perspective of that class that is most likely to be perpetuated. These are core perspectives "Poor whites" will see the world differently than will the moneyed class. So it is not a "race" thing. It is based in what you can *buy*, which establishes your status in society.

Perspectives are not simple. They are complex. And they are tacit. Not only is a person not usually aware of choosing or using a perspective on things, but they are not directly visible to others. We have to infer the perspective being ridden by what a person says and does. They are fundamental to the infrastructure that channels belief and feeling and actions. And yet we are so seldom aware of our own, and often wrong in accusing others – because we are most likely to accuse others of a perspective that we ourselves use to perform ourselves. We know that perspective in art and nature and judging others is part of the core that people use. But we are not usually on talking terms with our own perspectives.

For example, Samuel Johnson wrote, in *Rasselas*:

"Integrity without knowledge is weak and useless, and knowledge without integrity is dangerous and dreadful."

It is one thing to look upon the world with personal integrity. But if a person's supposed integrity is not well-informed, it is useless. Lots of people may go to school for many years to gain what we think of as "knowledge" in our culture. But this is most often used to get a better position or to fleece other people. If they have knowledge without integrity, they are dangerous. The world is increasingly being filled with dangerous people. They may be dangerous because they mislead us with their misleading perspectives. Or they may be dangerous because they want to eliminate (with guns or bombs) people who do not subscribe to the perspectives they subscribe to. They may simply be abusive because their only concerns in life are about themselves. Others are merely props in the dramas they create to star in as themselves. Integrity may involve something higher than one's immediate wants or needs. It is in small supply in our peculiar culture.

+++++

So core perspectives are what most people in a given culture have subscribed to, intentionally or inadvertently. They come to be a part of who you are through socialization. Some people are better or more socialized than other people. The difference might be seen as a difference in *conscience*. In a world where there are so many choices with respect to the subculture you might belong to, it is a term that means something other than it meant in prior generations. We live not in a moralistic society (which requires everyone to have an active conscience) but in a legalistic society. The perspective that alerts you to the difference is actually quite simple. A moralistic society requires you to do what you ought to do, and to refrain from doing what you ought not do. Traditional societies were mostly moralistic: You were socialized to avoid doing what you ought not do before you did it, and to think about what you ought to do before acting. You were to do your *duty*, no matter.

A legalistic society is one in which you are judged to have done wrong only after you had done wrong – and only if you got caught. Technically, you were speeding only if you got stopped for speeding. And you still have recourse in the courts to plead your case. You may have had a legally-acceptable reason for speeding. A moralistic society wants you not to speed because it is immoral to do so, so if you are a moral person, you don't. In a moral society, it may be a cultural perspective that killing innocent people is morally wrong. If you have a conscience about what is morally right or morally wrong, you are expected to do the right thing and avoid doing the wrong thing. In a legalistic society, it is wrong only if you can't (legally) argue your case. In terms of perspective, these are radically different societies. In a legalistic society, it is possible to do something that is morally wrong, but to do so conscience-free. For example, in a moralistic society, it is wrong to get rich off of other people's misfortunes. In a legalistic society, it is commonplace. An insurance salesperson may sell you a policy for more than you can afford that does not cover the circumstances stated or implied. Since it is *de rigueur* ("everybody" does it), it is not illegal. Our elected officials may not have done anything illegal, in spite of the fact that they are grossly immoral in their perspectives on you and the rest of the society. Getting rich by duping dupable people is not illegal. It is merely immoral, which matters little in a legalistic society. If these people had a good moral compass, they would not advantage themselves at a cost to their voters or the destiny of the nation. They would stop themselves from doing wrong. Otherwise, they are wrong only if they get caught after the damage is done, which (after the fact) may be too late.

The dilemma is that it takes a person having a good and working conscience to *make* a person with a good and working conscience. The perspectives they impose upon themselves and their worlds are very different for the moral person and the legalistic person. Add to that a permissive culture and a narcissistic one. Together, they provide a perspective that permits a person to do what they take to be justified if they abuse or shoot another person they don't like. Without a judge higher than they are, they are likely to be their own judge of their own personal feelings and actions. If parents raise children as the center of the universe, it is likely those children will think and feel and act as if they were the center of the universe. They may add up their "likes" for what they posted on the social media. But they may not like themselves. And this creates a problem for them personally and for the society collectively. Conscience is about consequences for the future. Legalisms are about precedent-setting processes. No "law" is held responsible for egregious outcomes. The costs become part of our GNP. The cost of the consequences are never deducted from the GNP.

This is but one of our culture's core perspectives. Another pervasive theme providing a near-universal perspective in our culture is what has been called the "Lone Ranger" syndrome. This is the belief (perhaps dating from "Little Red Riding Hood") that some ONE will come along and save us – either from ourselves or our own stupidity. We believe the President is going to save our country. We believe that it is the CEO who makes his/her organization successful, when it is actually the organization that makes the "leader" successful. This is eminently clear from history. We believe it is the conductor who makes the orchestra successful in concert. Not so. The chamber orchestra Orpheus has been around for 50+ years and won many awards for their performances, but has never had a conductor. We like to believe that it is the coach who more or less single-handedly makes a winning football team. So if he or she doesn't have a winning season or two, they get fired and a new coach is put in place. What we know about CEOs is that their contribution to the success or failure of an organization is only about 5% of what is required. We don't change our minds about this when the evidence is clear and weighty. We simply ignore the facts in order to cling to our perspective that this is so. The best and worthiest leaders know this is so, and they say so. The Lone Ranger (or these days some other super-hero) is a mythical, not a real, character. We believe the myth because we grew up on it, not because it is in any sense true. Is it our need to be saved from ourselves by what we believe to be (our perspective) a superhero? Why would this be so strong in an egalitarian democracy which is of the people, by the people, and for the people?

Or is it just testimony to the fact that myths (or beliefs) are stronger than "facts"?

Science and "scientists" have their own perspective. Since that perspective is becoming hegemonic in our society, perhaps we should examine that more carefully. That scientists know more than we do and have an open road to "reality," we should perhaps note that their perspective is just as subjective as our own. Some "scientizers" may claim objectivity. But even quantum physicists understand that there are no exploratory tools that will tell them what's out there in their world. They can only create instruments for what they are looking for. Like all the rest of us, they can't see the world as it *is*. They can only see the world as *they* are. For the leading-edge physicists, the baffling question is that when they measure something, it is there. But is it there when it is not being measured? Is a loved one the same person when he or she is somewhere else, doing other things? How could you *know*? Science calls for just as much faith as love does – or as believing in a god does. As William James wrote in the title essay of *The Will to Believe:*

> *"A fact [may] not come at all unless a preliminary faith exists in its coming.*...Faith in a fact can help create the fact."

In other words, science does not "discover" the facts or the truth of anything. It finds a way of measuring what their faith says is out there to be measured. A composer has faith in the way he or she has put the notes together. An artist has faith that if they do this or that with their painting, it will move people as they had hoped. We live by prophecy and faith, not by the facts. Love is like that. Life is like that. If science is not, it is because they operate by a very different perspective. If scientists themselves live by the facts they explain to the rest of us, there is little evidence. Like the rest of us, their faith in gravity is boundless. But theirs is a core perspective taking over more of our cultural perspectives.

+++++

There is something about humans in general – and perhaps people in our own culture especially – that makes *stories* more compelling than any facts. And the more dramatic those stories are, the more compelling they are. The experts at this are those who create and design our commercial advertising...and our neighborhood gossips. By comparison, even our best novelists and playwrights are less influential. Every journalist knows that a "human-interest" story is more impactful than mere facts or statistics. We are socialized by the stories our parents tell, and by the stories our peers tell. They may be entertaining, but that doesn't preclude their being carriers of the core perspectives of our culture. They may be dark or horrific, but that doesn't preclude their being carriers of our cultural core perspectives. Dilbert or Seinfeld may be ironic or satirical, but that does not mean that our consumption of them doesn't influence us in the direction of the core perspectives carried in their themes and actions. And we know that Lucy is going to take the football away at the last moment so that Charlie Brown falls from his own impetus. But we have all been betrayed by those we *trusted*. And that segment raises a fundamental issue in any society – whom can I trust?

And how do I determine that? Or can there be such a thing as trust if there is no such thing as betrayal (of that trust)? Lovers trust in faithfulness. But when shouldn't they? Your doctor may be implying, "Trust me, I'm a doctor." But she's only guessing. If she guesses wrong, you may pay for it with your life. But here we are, in the middle of *that* story. Does it make a difference whose perspective controls the process in that story? Then there are the stories that commercial advertisers bombard us with 24/7. Their stories, because they have people in them and are usually animated or quite dramatic, are compelling – if consumed. Their stories are either explicit or implied. Either way, they either refract or alter one or more of our cultural core perspectives. So when Willa Cather wrote, in *O Pioneers*:

> *"There are only two or three human stories, and they go on repeating themselves as fiercely as if they had never happened before."*

She was intimating that there are very few fundamental stories, and that our story is a variation on the plot. The basic story is that you are born, you live your life, and then you die. All the rest is a variation on that plot. There is no end to the possible variations on that plot. Or, another may be that there is a likeable protagonist who is trying to accomplish something in his or her life, and the story is about the obstacles that occur that deter the protagonist from his goal (the Romeo and Juliet story). The ready implication is that the world does not conspire to assist you in achieving your desires. In his Noble Prize speech in 1950, William Faulkner projected the writer as playing god:

"He [the writer] must teach himself that the basest of all things is to be afraid; and, teaching himself that, forget it forever, leaving no room in his workshop for anything but the old verities and truths of the heart, the old universal truths lacking which any story is ephemeral and doomed – love and honor and pity and pride and compassion and sacrifice."

This is his perspective on his stories, of course. But it is perhaps at the same time a perspective on how life ought to be lived – to live as if all were possible, his designations but examples. Many of the themes in modern times are related to *envy*. If you did this or had that, those in your social circle would be envious. And this would raise your status until you are outdone by someone else in your social circles and ended up being envious of that other person – the price to be paid when envy is a core perspective in your culture, just as pride may be. If you use this toothpaste I'm holding in my hand, the paid endorser says, your teeth will be enviably whiter than anyone who beholds you. We would all like our lives to be stories that are not ephemeral and doomed. But we may not be willing to pay the price of not being "afraid." It is our mental dragons that keep us from playing our lives as we imagine we should. We fear the virtual as much (or more?) than the real? It's likely that Faulkner was talking about the little fears we have every day that keep us from being who we ought to (or even want to) be. We fear the loss of what has become familiar to us – like our personal identities.

We read stories. We watch stories. We hear stories. We tell stories. Yet the only stories that move us are the ones we adapt in our own lives. It was Horace (65-8 B.C.) who perhaps offered the best reason for being open to other stories and learning from them:

"The story's about you."

If it is not about you or useful to you, what would be the reason for consuming it? The main story in your life is the story of your life. We compose it as we go from day to day. The life you can't compose for your life is a life you cannot have. It's what you learn from stories that matters, not their diversionary value. People who can't learn from consuming stories or telling them is a person who is starving his or her spirit. It is stories that can create and recreate us, not facts. Facts may be a part of some story or other. But facts are not the story. Even a collection of facts – called "statistics" – is not a story. A story might be made of them. But story is a human thing. Stories – as indispensable as they are – are about life and living. The facts may propel a story, but they are not the story. Aesop understood. The characters may be animals, but if the story moves the reader or listener, it is a story about his or her life.

+++++

Statistics are often interesting, but essentially lifeless. The "average" foot size for your demographic may be of some trivial interest. But few people would want to be average enough to add to their feet or cut some off. It may be that more people in your demographic commit suicide than in the larger society. But that doesn't translate into a lemming-like rush to suicide. More people in your demographic may be dead. But that will be unlikely to lead you to where they have gone. We have heard a lot about "peer pressure" in the last century or so. But people deal with the peers that surround them, not with statistics *about* them. If you are reading or watching television, it is likely that the most compelling influence is anecdotal – that is, that it is about a particular person. Of the many thousands of photographs to come out of the wars in the mid-East, the one that grabbed the most attention was of a single Afghan girl. The story may be about a catastrophe of major scope. But it doesn't seem to affect us much until it is dramatized in its effect on one person.

What we can gather from this is that most of our learning from stories come either from the story-teller herself, or from the characters she has created. There are novels about historical epochs or about a near-universal perspective on some event. But most novels are about a person or two, and most stories are formulaic. It is the drama and the risk involved that capture our attention. That may be because we have less and less fulfilling drama in our personal lives. It is in combat that people come fully alive, not in reading about it or calculating the statistics about it. We are hungry for drama in our lives. And if we don't get enough of it to satisfy our hunger, we create it. Hate is an alternative to love for getting our imaginations and our adrenalin running. Tell me a story means stir my feelings. At this, no one succeeds better than commercial advertisers. It is the story implicit in the commercials that we feed on. And then, if they become boring, we turn to the drama choices we have on television. The juiciest tabloid in our lives may be the local rumor mill, since the "stars" are either people we know, or those we know from stories told about them. We may have more lurid interest in our favorite celebrities than we have in our increasingly dull spouses or lovers.

Why this should be so has everything to do with the core perspectives that have become a part of who we are in our culture. We wouldn't have to become disenchanted with our lovers or our spouses. It's just a superordinate story that we unwittingly act out in our own lives because it is so familiar to us. Salvador Dali said that *So little of what could happen does happen.* We invent and consume stories to enhance the dullness in our lives. Consult the tabloids.

+++++

Our core perspectives lead us into ways of living our lives – both individually and collectively. In *The News: A User's Manual*, the popular British writer Alain de Botton made this observation:

> *"There is a peculiar, though undeniable, benefit to be found in exposure to the sufferings of strangers.... This may be because we are all, somewhere within us, uncomfortably sad and disappointed. We harbour, quietly, a lot of darkness. At the same time, we live in societies that ceaselessly promote images of ambition and happiness, of thriving relationships, lucrative careers and successful endeavours, most of which lie painfully out of our reach."*

If this is true, then there is an underlying and core perspective that leads us to perform our lives in the spirit of optimistic pessimism. It was once reported that black women buy more cosmetics than white women. At that time, the models were mostly all white. If de Botton is right, our futures have to do with hope. Our pasts, with regret. Indeed, we are saddened by lives that do not turn out as we would have them turn out. We are disappointed in our pasts, to the point that we don't even have much hope for the future. Is this the case because of our genes? Is this the case because it just is? Is this the case because we have exposed ourselves to too many stories (even from your local gossip) about this sort of sadness and disappointment? Or is this the case because the longer we are alive, the more our pasts count for our present circumstances, and the less our hopes for the future count for our present. If so, the core perspective that our past determines our present and our present determines our future leads us to play our lives this way.

Would we have to? No. Do we have to because our core perspective on such things leads us to believe we have to? Possibly. Our perspectives determine how we think, thus who we *are,* and thus what we do. They don't "tell" us what to do. They frame and parameter our lives just because they are at the core of who we are – how we look at things and how we are led to think and feel about our circumstances. We take them as "givens." We stand on them, unexamined as they are, to be who we are in our worlds.

It's difficult to change our foundations when we have to stand on them in order to do so.

> *"Years steal*
> *Fire from the mind as vigor from the limb; And*
> *life's enchanted cup but sparkles near the brim."*
>
> --George Gordon, Lord Byron

Perspective 4

Relevance

There are two kinds of relevance that we should be curious to explore here:

1. There is *what, or who, is relevant* to you at any moment;

2. And then there is *to what, or to whom,* are you *relevant* in your life?

It is largely our perspectives on ourselves and our worlds that channel whatever attention we pay to what is going on inside or outside of us. If you are hungry, anything that hints of food may get your attention. If you are looking for your car keys, most of the rest of the world is shut out temporarily. If you are in an art museum, one might assume you would be looking at what is on display on the walls of the museum. But some people gather there just to socialize. They obviously have a different perspective on art and art museums. If you are driving, you should probably be giving your attention to what other drivers are doing. But some people use their commute to finish their personal getting ready for work. Others listen to music. Still others listen to the news. There will always be those who are simply bored by the passing scenes. There are multiple perspectives at play, some accounting for car crashes, others putting the driver on autopilot to kill the time required to traverse the space between here and there. There are always many different perspectives at play in our private and social lives. There are also many different consequences as they intermingle in almost everything we do.

Relevance is a condition that affects every person's psychological and social life. It gets a thorough exploration in my book *Relevance* as it applies to people's lives – from now through to the end. Here, we want to focus on what is relevant to us and why, and even more importantly, to focus on how relevant we feel we are to the larger world, and how vital that is to our lives in all kind of ways.

+++++

Let us consider the first of these types of relevance: what is relevant to us at any juncture in our lives?

It should by now be obvious that the dominant claim on our perceptions of the world is our perspective on things. The perspective having hegemonic priority at any moment will be the one that determines what will be most relevant to us at that moment. A moment before or a moment later may enable and constrain a different perception of what's relevant at *that* moment. If in pain, we are likely to focus on that. If some scenery outside our window is compelling, we are likely to focus on that.

If something smells particularly good or bad, that will grab our attention. Loud noises will distract, soft music may beckon our attention. A person who appeals to us will draw attention, as will a person we consider to be ugly. For some people, an email received or a call coming in may take precedence over any other concerns. And, above all, what's going on with you in terms of your mental machinations will ultimately determine what you will pay attention to. Ortega Y. Gasset made this observation:

> "Tell me to what you pay attention and I will tell you who you are."

Who we "are," of course, is given in how our minds work. We are no more than what our unique minds are capable of. Perceiving (or paying attention to someone or something) is fundamental to the processes of communication – acquiring something that is meaningful to us. And our minds and how we communicate (inwardly or outwardly) are two aspects of the same thing. So Gasset is reminding us of the obvious: that how we take the world-into-account and how *we* intend to be taken-into-account by that world when we talk or comport ourselves in that world reveals the way our minds work. We *are* the way our minds work. And the core proclivities there are our perspectives on ourselves and the worlds in which we are ourselves. Just keep in mind that our senses are primarily for the purpose of acquiring information from outside ourselves, not for being seen or heard.

It's interesting that Gasset doesn't lay the judgment on the person. If an outsider (Gasset) could tell us who we are by observing what we pay attention to, why couldn't we do this for ourselves? We *could,* perhaps. But why is it so few people – who say they are not happy with their lives – use their own capacity to "see" who they are and thus what they might need to change in order to be someone more to their liking? Could it be that they never learned that perspective on their own lives? What special capacity of his is Gasset referring to? Is he saying that he can do this because he is not the person he is observing? Does being an outsider enable one to do this? If so, couldn't the person de-center herself and see herself as others do? Others apparently have an advantaged perspective on us. Why couldn't we have the same kind of advantage by looking upon ourselves as others see us? A person who can see herself (a contrary perspective) as others do might see why she is seen by those others as not likable. Do we avoid this because we don't want to know? Or do we avoid it because – in spite of saying we are not entirely satisfied with our lives – we believe we can't change? Most people seem to have the kinds of minds that permit them to be somewhat dissatisfied with the way their lives have gone or are going but, at the same time, being actively resistant to doing anything about it. Why do we harbor such perverse perspectives? One of the questions Ortega's terse observation might lead to is this: Why do we "see" the world from the point of view of who we "are" rather than who we would like to be? Is it solely because the culture and the subcultures in which we become socialized encourage this kind of solipsism? Even if they engendered such perspectives in us, why would we be unwilling to sacrifice the life we have for a life having more efficacious perspectives? Why is it we readily adapt ourselves to certain perspectives but seem reluctant to trade those for better ones? There is no such thing as an ideal perspective. But there undeniably are human ideals. If we could imagine a better life than the one we have, what is holding us back? Epictetus said:

> *"First, say to yourself what you would be; then do what you have to do."*

What kind of perspective would you need to exercise on yourself and your world to take that as your mantra in life? Seems basic, and as simply put as it could be. But in this complex world we inhabit, are we looking for something more complex? William James, sometimes referred to as the father of American psychology, taught and wrote from much the same perspective. Yet, that kind of perspective seems to have fallen out of favor in modern psychology. Why? It's obviously not new. And if it's not new, it may have little or no relevance?

+++++

What is relevant to us at any moment is something that, or someone who, has immediate meaning to us. Whatever its many other functions may be, the basic stuff of the mind is *meaning*. So our first perspective on the world is whatever about that world is meaningful to a given person. The second perspective is whatever vested interest we have in what is going on. For example, we have a vested interest in our possessions. We have a vested interest in our relationships with others. We have a vested interest in whether or not we are fashionable given the ever-changing fashions in dress, looks, coiffures, etc. We have a vested interest in anything that might bear upon how we think we should play our day, or our life. So we are watchers of "the news." We seem to have a lurid interest in plane crashes or spectacular car crashes, wars, pestilence, details about our celebrities' lives and lifestyles, and other "newsworthy" events, like the old saw about what constitutes news-worthiness, **"Man Bites Dog."** We think we need to know about this stuff. But since most people don't seem to have a clue about what they might *need* to know, they collect whatever is on offer on "the news," letting the people who broadcast the news for money decide for them. It has some logic, in our culture. What is relevant in general appears to be what people in general believe is relevant – like a huge but anonymous television audience. Not knowing what we need to know puts us together with thousands of other people who don't know what they need to know. So we consume what they consume, in case we are stuck in some meaningless conversation with them. What is relevant personally is either something that, or someone who, confirms who I think I am in this world. Or it is something that puts my comfort-zone life in jeopardy? From the average person's point of view (or perspective) in our peculiar culture, he or she is the most relevant person on earth. So it's what's going on with them that is most relevant. If it's not about them, it is likely to have comparatively very little relevance for them. If you want to know what is relevant to any person at any moment in time or longer term, watch what they pay attention to. If they are okay with very little return on their attention (ROA), then you can make a fairly good guess about just how relevant something was to them.

What people are most likely to be exposed to, whether in person or via the media, is *advice*. The more relevant to their lives it might be, the more they avoid or dismiss it. The less relevant it might be to improve the quality of their lives, the more appetite they have for it. This may be no more than the potency of the status quo is our lives. Whatever trajectory in life we happen to be on is the status quo, and if the advice reinforces the status quo we welcome it. Whatever doesn't reinforce our personal status quo is presumed to require change. So it is considered far less relevant and maybe not at all relevant. As Lord Chesterfield averred:

> *"Advice is seldom welcome, and those who need it*
> *the most, like it the least."*

Again, this adversity should probably be attributed to the fact that people take what is in their perspective on things to be reality. And they are reluctant to change the status quo, no matter how advantageous to them it might be. So we needn't blame people for being "resistant" to change. It's just the way it is. They are protecting their *personal* status quo.

When a perspective seems to be working, people stick with it. When it seems not to be working, most people tend to blame the world outside of them – maybe not rationally, but perspectives (like all kinds of mental algorithms) usually take precedence over any facts. The "facts" are usually brought to the fore by someone else. One's channeling perspectives may preclude one from seeing certain adverse details as relevant. *So, what is relevant to whom, given what perspective?* The tricky thing about relevance is that other people have to deduce it from what a person pays attention to – and guessing as well why. And the person to whom something is relevant is often surprised by what grabbed his or her attention. And, often, they don't care. Paying attention to something is better than staring at a blank wall. "Waiting rooms" typically have some magazines or other material to pay attention to. Otherwise, it's either looking at the other patients (which is not social protocol), or at the wall.

What's relevant to certain people at certain times may be wayward. But it has consequences for that person and thus, ultimately, for the society. Are people responsible for the consequences of what is relevant to them from time to time? In our medical-pharmaceutical-welfare society, it seems less and less so. People are free to choose what is relevant *to them*, whether that be good for them or bad for them. We have pills for being active beyond the norm at the time, and we have pills for being too inactive, or depressed. We have pills to counteract the effects of those pills. We have pills to counteract the ill effects of the counteractive pills. So what's the problem? Could it be that what is fashionable (or normative) will be done, no matter the consequences? And we mustn't forget that relevance is tacit (felt), rarely corporeal.

And if you like the paradoxes there, consider the research which suggests that the people who are most immune to the advice *they* need are the same people who are ready, willing, and able to give other people advice whether they ask for it or not. A pithy comment by Evan Esar makes the point well:

> *"Advice is an opinion given by someone who can't use it to someone who won't."*

It's as if we were overflowing with advice that we have no use for and therefore distributed it freely to other people who won't (or can't) make use of it. Casual conversations are often like that. Given that one's bin of good intentions is full, the excess is freely distributed. That the supply outpaces the demand may in turn suggest that people in general do not know what they *need* to know. So they imbibe whatever comes along. It might be useful for the next casual conversation. At least one's voice mail will reject everything beyond its storage capacity, even if the rejected message was about mandatory evacuation, or about some critical lab reports. The digital world may be believed to make us smarter. But no smart phone can tell you what you *need* to know. It can only display what is in the archives. Perspectives are like that. They can bring you only what they are capable of bringing you. They cannot bring you what *you* need to know. What is relevant to you is a function of you, not of what might potentially be relevant to you. Your life carries with it some indivisible responsibilities. If you don't know what is relevant – to *you* – that part of your life will go missing.

+++++

The *second* of these two kinds of relevance is, in most respects, far more important. People desperately need to be relevant to others, and thus to the larger world. It is vital to our existence. Babies die without it. Adults do too, but they pay for it by a diminished sense life. They pay for it in sickness of mind and spirit, for which there are no third-party-payer pills. They pay for it in not belonging to something that is bigger than they are. To lose one's relevance to the larger world, or to the only people one knows, is to lose one's sense of identity and well-being.

Such people go emotionally distraught. Mothers are relevant, if only to their babies. Plumbers are relevant to the workings of everyday. Farmers are relevant.

Doctors and lawyers *can* be relevant, as can a highway patrol officer. The best teachers can be relevant to their pupils. The best (or worst) pupils can be relevant to their teachers. Auto fix-it places can be relevant, but only if something goes wrong with your car. "Space" is relevant, but mostly only to an astronaut and the engineers who outfit their vehicles. Are astronauts relevant to space? Therein lies the difference between what is relevant to whom, and to whom or to what one is relevant.

One's relevance *to* someone or something is a feeling that is sourced in a relationship. When the relationship goes, the feeling of relevance goes with it. If you go to the ER, you are relevant to the people who tend you there. But you will be relevant to them only so long as you are there. And, in general, only so long as they are getting paid for their services; it's their "job." It seems that this is one reason why people go to the ER: they are apparently desperate to have the feeling that they are relevant to something/someone outside of themselves. You are relevant to the people at the auto fix-it place, but only so long as you are a paying customer. If you are not, you are not welcome there. As a mother, you are relevant to your baby – but only until your baby isn't so needful. Then some sort of post-partum depression may set in. If you had a "job" at the same place for most of your life, and you retired or got fired, you will feel a sudden loss of relevance to the larger world. You are dispensable – no longer a needed cog in the machinery. If your spouse dies after many years, you will feel a loss of relevance to the world because you are no longer relevant as a spouse. If your peers at school reject you, you may feel alienated – no longer relevant to that social world outside yourself. If your friends of many years move away, you may try to keep in touch as before, but it isn't the same. You will feel a loss. The loss is your feelings of no longer being so relevant to those now-distant friends. You may feel relevant to your favorite celebrities, but they won't have much of a sense of being relevant to you until large numbers of you cease to pay for their performances or their products. Every social group organizes around status. If you lose your status, you lose your sense of being so relevant to those who deferred to your status. So status is a measure of relevance *to* others, to the larger social world outside yourself. If someone loved you, you felt relevant to that person and thus to the rest of the world. If they cease to care one way or the other about you, you will suffer the loss of that sense of relevance. You may be better off. But relevance trumps our feelings about such things every time.

The whole of psychology could be built on the concept of *relevance*, which points us in the direction of meaning. We are created in relationships. It is relationship that fulfills our vital need for meaning in our lives. Different relationships (or the lack or loss thereof) spawn different perspectives on things. And it is those perspectives from which our feelings derive. Alter those perspectives and you alter your feelings about things. As Emerson wrote in his *Journal* (December 20, 1822):

> *"To different minds, the same world is a hell, and a heaven."*

If that is where Freud got his notion that in their talking, people can create their own heavens and hells we can never know. The point is that different perspectives create different worlds, both personally and collectively. We live in the worlds made possible or impossible given our perspectives on things. Those are virtual worlds. We can't talk about any "real" world, but only our perspectives on it (our interpretations of it). All human perspectives come with the feelings that are assumed to go with them, according to the culture or subcultures in which we are socialized. Those feelings, expressed or imbibed, are laden with certain meanings ... to the person having them or observing others. What we "see" are the feelings we would have if in that situation. The point is this:

> *For whatever reason, when a person experiences a loss of relevance, that person's emotional and physical health are now in jeopardy.*

We see this most notably as people age. Aging may bring its physical or biological aches and pains. Aging also brings the despair of those who like to look at themselves in the mirror. When they begin to look old to themselves, they begin to act as if they were old. But aging also brings with it in most cases a sense of loss of relevance to the larger society. As Eleanor Roosevelt said, *"When you cease to make a contribution, you begin to die."* Increasingly, most people's lives today don't make much of a contribution beyond their small social circles. They did, at one time, when every person was relevant to the whole – as on self-sufficient farms. To live a life without a purpose is almost not to have lived at all. To live a life without a *worthy* purpose is to be like flotsam on the sea of humanity. Even making a contribution to oneself may be worthy. Making a contribution to others (or to the destiny of the society) can be worthier.

It may not be a life or death circumstance. But the presence or absence of relevance to the larger whole can be. People die of loneliness – that is, of their feelings of not being, or no longer being, relevant to the causes of others. For their own mental and physical health, people want to feel relevant to something larger than themselves – and this may be possible only if they are in some vital sense relevant to the larger world beyond themselves. It's difficult to know what a rock fan's paid ticket of admission may contribute to the larger world. In a culture where entertainment is the most pursued leisure time activity, the price of progress may be the loss of relevance. People have been known to kill large numbers of other people just to get the publicity that makes them relevant, however fleeting, in the media. Suicide bombers can make an immediate contribution to the world of the news. And if the world of the news is the world most people live in, then indeed suicide bombers have become relevant to their audiences worldwide. If the news portrays what we have to look forward to, then Emerson may have been wrong: That "same world" begins to look less and less like a heaven anyone you know would want to live in.

We live in a culture of diminishing responsibility for the *consequences* of one's personal choices. For example, a person could choose to kill someone, but in court attribute what happened to temporary insanity. A person could choose to get drunk (permissible). But the same person could choose to drive his vehicle while drunk. It is not illegal to make those choices. It is only illegal if he gets caught on a charge of DUI, accident or not. The DUI was his choice. Can he be charged for the consequences of DUI, or does "under the influence" become the culprit?

Or, let's say a person decides to learn how to smoke cigarettes (and go through the physiological distress that accompanies learning how), and later develops some smoking-related disease. Why is it that the cigarettes get the blame and not the smoker? If a person overeats and thereby invites certain diseases, is the food to be blamed? In a narcissistic culture such as our own, we seem to have increasingly shifted the blame for the circumstances over time onto something other than the person who made the choice. George Bernard Shaw would certainly not be seen as having a perspective on such things that would jibe with the pop-culture perspective. In *Mrs. Warren's Profession*, Shaw wrote:

> *"People are always blaming their circumstances*
> *for what they are. I don't believe in circumstances.*
> *The people who get on in this world are the people*
> *who get up and look for the circumstances they*
> *want and, if they can't find them, make them."*

In other words, the perspective coming from the pop culture is more like,

"I have a right to do as I damn well please. Let someone else clean up the consequences." It has been becoming more so in the years since 1893. Shaw expresses this elsewhere (in *Man and Superman*) as being *"a feverish selfish little clod of ailments and grievances complaining that the world will not devote itself to making you happy."* That wouldn't include everyone – but seemingly a growing number of our society's constituents.

We are a welfare and entitlement society – meaning also that foreign laborers take jobs no young American seems to want (preferring to move back home where life was easy). Still, this perspective is almost wholly at odds with the pop culture perspective. And it does seem to be the case that we spend more for "health" care than any other nation, but still have more illness. Two questions emerge: How could Shaw have been so prescient? And where did the perspective come from that the outside *world* is obligated to devote itself to making us happy and healthy?

Our founding fathers wrote about "the pursuit of happiness" – not society's obligation to provide happiness to all. Where did that perspective come from? It is clear that some social movements change things and some do not. JFK said, "Ask not what your country can do for you; ask what you can do for your country" (having copped this from Oliver Wendell Holmes without attribution). It sounds good and maybe gets votes. But you would not find many people in this country who have taken that sage advice. Again, the pop culture, being as pervasive as it is in this digital age, is a very potent force when it comes to popular perspectives on how to live life. That was what philosophy was all about in earlier times. But these days we are more likely to be swayed by what our media celebrities say. Or what those whose favor we are currying have to say about how to live a more relevant life. If we fail to take care of our society, it cannot take care of us. Selfishly, we may expect so. But the fundament is that we create or buy-into the perspectives by which we channel our lives. The perspectives we garner from our pop culture are perspectives that people have put there. No society is self-correcting (as Jared Diamond has compellingly demonstrated in his work). If there is to be a course correction – a correction in perspective – it will have to come from us. Change is easy to talk about in the abstract. But when it appears to involve our making any changes, we resist. We are relevant because of the way we are, not the way we might be after our perspectives have changed. To change, individuals would have to give up their present identity and lifestyle in order to gain another, perhaps better, one. If our personal and collective histories are any evidence, this is either unlikely to happen, or to happen so slowly that we don't notice it. There is no rational solution to an irrational situation.

Which brings us around to the point to be made: that any loss of a feeling of *relevance* to the larger whole alienates a person not just from the larger whole, but places one's very sense of self in jeopardy. To be relevant to the larger whole requires being relevant to those who have a vested interest in the way it works at present. If the world will not devote itself to making any of us happy, wherein lies the remedy? Obviously not with any society. "Society" is an abstraction. It has no feelings. And just as obviously, people who have no transcending cause or purpose in life but depend upon society to take care of them are living in an asymmetrical relationship. It is in doing good for others that one makes his or her contribution to society (ancient wisdom). If a person does not *belong* to a social group where the relationship is mutual, or if that person does not *belong* to his or her cause or purpose in life, then that person is alienated from himself or herself. If you are not relevant to the larger whole in this sense, you will begin to develop a truncated feeling of loss of self, which will have both psychological and physical consequences. It bears repeating: We emerge in our relationships with others, and they are the source of what perpetuates our feelings of personal identity. Lose those, and you begin to lose everything. You cease to be relevant to anyone or anything in the worlds you inhabit.

+++++

Relevance requires *belonging to* someone or something in your world. If you *belong* to your cause and purpose it life, that will suffice for some – it will suffice for those who can sustain themselves in their own solitude. If you have a compelling cause and purpose in life, you won't be spending much of your life with crowds, either in person or on some digital device. Our pop-cultural perspective is that people "need" people. There's even a popular song that has that title. Having a cause and purpose in life seemingly makes up for a lot of that "need" for constant contact with other people (who seem to be similarly without any particular purpose in life). The less purposeful one is, the more need he or she has for being with and like other people. Most people haven't got what it takes to be devoted to a cause and purpose in life. Needing to fulfill a worthy cause in life and needing to be in contact with other people constantly during one's waking hours are, it seems, mutually exclusive.

+++++

Relevance is a subjective state of mind. The feelings of contribution that often attend that state of mind are also subjective. They are mostly psychosocial in source and destination. We feel good about being relevant to others. If there is a loss of relevance, for any reason, we begin to feel bereft. Being relevant to the larger world affects how relevant one can feel to herself. Losing that sense of relevance to the larger world can be critical to one's mental and physical health. Having an indispensable role at work or family can lead one to feel relevant to the larger world. Losing those for any reason can lead the person to a diminished sense of the worthiness of her life. It should be fundamental to any treatment of an infant or an aging person. There has been much said over the years about what is "relevant" to persons or a person. But very little (actually, almost nothing) has been said about the far more vital condition of what or whom a person is relevant TO.

Either way involves a perspective that may be efficacious or not. Loss of relevance to the larger society is a precursor to many of the mental and physical degeneration "diseases" that occur as people age, or as they become marginalized at any age. And it is *that* perspective that we have explored in this chapter. People who feel relevant to the larger whole have a very different perspective on themselves and their worlds than do people who (for any reason) have begun to lose their sense of *relevance to* the world outside themselves. A sense of relevance – or a sense of the loss of relevance – to the larger world may be found to be fundamental to the mental and physical health of people who are aging. But it can happen at any age. It is a psychosocial dysfunction, not a biological one. To treat it as the latter may in many instances exacerbate the problem.

There is no pill for the feelings that usually accompany any loss of relevance. A person often has a potent sense of relevance to his or her perspectives on life and self. Some people are willing to die rather than change their perspectives. Heavy smokers have been known to do just that. Some people are willing to risk their lives at war in order to get other people to change their perspectives. But "our" perspectives are a part of who we are. Giving up or changing one's perspectives often means changing who one is. It is rarely done volitionally. If who or what one is relevant *to* changes, then one changes out of necessity. Where one's personal perspectives are concerned, they function much like longstanding ideologies. And it is easy to observe that ideologies usually trump even common sense. Perspectives are vitally relevant. A person is relevant to his or her perspective, and the human struggles that history records have most often been struggles for hegemony of perspective. If a new scientific theory comes along, those whose identities have been entwined with an existing theory will resist it. It is only the next generation that might embrace it.

The people around us see us in 3-D. Using a mirror, we can only see ourselves in two dimensions. Comprehension is at stake. It is our explanations (our perspectives) that enable comprehension. Changing our perspectives means changing our ways of comprehending ourselves and our worlds. Relevance constitutes the tectonics both of personal life and the life of the society. It is far too important a psychological and social function to be ignored. As a cultural perspective, that may not happen in your lifetime. But if you make it a core part of your perspective on yourself and your world, you will have a better life and a better world.

What is relevant to you is what you therefore give your attention. If you have a worthy cause and purpose in life you will then choose what is relevant to you very strategically. Whether that be people or events or things, what is relevant to you is what will determine your perspective on yourself and that world. And that will bear mightily on the life you can have in your lifetime.

That's the minor part of it. The major part of it – the part that most bears upon the quality of your life and your longevity is this: your relevance *to* the larger world. If you are making worthy contributions, you will feel relevant. If you are not, you won't. The less relevant to the larger world you are, or feel you are, the most negative consequences for your life – e.g., depression, anger, frustration, and a sense of alienation, with all of the mental and physical consequences that result from the sense of declining relevance.

As Eleanor Roosevelt rightly admonished:

> *"When you cease to make a contribution, you begin to die."*

That is, when you cease being *relevant* to the world beyond you?

> *"Everything we see is a perspective, not the truth."*

> --Marcus Aurelius

Perspective 5

How We Think about Things

We like to assume we *can* think. But most of what passes for thinking by most people is merely a regurgitation of something they've heard, seen, or read. Henry Ford quipped that thinking is one of the hardest things there is to do. And, he continued, that's the reason why so few people ever learn how to think. So what that means is that most people are stuck with the perspectives they absorb from the people they most regularly hang out with. A perspective that is not thoughtfully chosen to further one's cause and purpose in life is at best a second-hand one. People who can't really think have minds full of the current clichés of the social networks they belong to. They speak in clichés, the filters at work when they hear or read something are clichés, and they see the world in terms of familiar clichés. They are for the most part good people. But they speak in a mediocre vernacular which dissolves them into mediocrity. And a mediocre way of working or of talking leads them into mediocrity. They understand only that world which is familiar to them. They are not curious about much of anything. Reading beyond what they regularly read is hard for them. They feel offended by people who talk or read in a vernacular which is "above" them. They avoid situations that might require thinking. And they have a prejudice – actually a dislike – for people who can think. They are carried downstream by the flotsam of their everyday lives. They are victims of the experts and of people who are more articulate than they are. They choose gatherings of people who are like they are. They become anonymous members of what have been called the "masses." They inhabit a more or less literal world of their own making. They do not dream of a better life. They are content to be militantly "average." The perspective of mediocrity is the most hegemonic perspective in our culture.

This has probably always been the case. People like to be like other people. People like to be with people who are like they are. People prefer to be with other people whose perspectives are like theirs. Our educational system does not teach people how to think. It teaches them how to let others do their thinking for them. One could argue that there is nothing wrong with this – since it seems to have been the way things are since the beginning of human history. But there may be one thing wrong with it. It is that people who can't think for themselves are proselytizers. Perhaps without even intending to, people who can't think try to seduce others to be like they are. Thinkers might also try to seduce others to be like they are. But they are too few to make much of a difference. Meanwhile, mediocrity increases exponentially.

Metaphorically, mediocrity functions as social gravity much like physical gravity. We don't know exactly why or what it is, but we see its effects every day. So it is *that* perspective that is taking over our culture. In this chapter, we will want to explore what that means for you today…and for your society how that bears on your future and that of your progeny.

+++++

The first thing to understand about your thinking is that it is cumulative. As each day passes, you will be able to think about the things that need thinking about only as well as your past thoughts make possible. This has been known from ancient times. For example, in *The Dhammapada* (3rd century B.C.E. and representing the "scriptures" of the Buddha) there are these lines:

"What we are today comes from our thoughts of yesterday, and our present thoughts build our life of tomorrow: our life is the creation of the mind."

Since the Buddha intended his sayings as a way of making a rightful path in life, there are at least two perspectives worth our attention here:

1. One is that we become what we think about all day. What we think about today determines what we will become tomorrow. The point here is that thoughts are born of previous thoughts. We can only have the thoughts that our previous thoughts enable.

2. The other is that one's life and one's mind are two aspects of the same thing. Life is created consciously in the thoughts we have about it. Emerson put it more modernly: *"Life consists of what [a person] is thinking all day."* Think different thoughts and you live in a different world. Live in a different world and you have a different life.

In our peculiar culture, we may like to believe that if we apprehend a person or a thing, we understand that person or that thing. Yet eyewitness accounts of a crime are often contradictory. Kurosawa captured this nicely in his film, *Rashomon*. No two people see the "same" thing in the same way. Our minds are not creations of any real world. They are the creations of how we talk about things – about the virtual reality we create in talking about things. We are not usually present when others are creating our reputations – their interpretations of us.

How we see ourselves and how others see us are two different things. What we think of ourselves and what others think of us are two different perspectives. The Spanish have a proverb: *To speak of bulls is not the same thing as to be in the bullring.* You can't get gored by words. On the other hand, our words are our reality. A surgeon carries out a surgical procedure. The person undergoing the procedure has a body that experiences the surgery, and it is that person that has to live with the after effects. What went on meant quite different things to the surgeon and her patient. We like to think we are talking about the same thing. But we are not. We are talking about our perspective, our interpretation, of whatever we're talking about. If the conversationalists are French, and you are not fluent in French, it's unlikely that you will understand what they are talking about. If they are speaking English, you most likely will not really understand what they mean by what they say, but you pretend to and thus move things along. There is a children's ditty about a cow that jumped over the moon. What does that *mean*? We know how to recite many clichés, such as "I love you," but we don't know exactly what that means – whether we say it or hear it. Our lives are not about what it means, but about getting on with whatever is going on. We are not a thoughtful bunch, we moderns.

We think, if at all, with our perspectives and our beliefs – or our opinions, as Marcus Aurelius said. We like to think that we are thinking about the realities of the world we inhabit. But we aren't. The best we can do is to contemplate what we take to be real because we can talk about it. What is beyond your comprehension is what you cannot talk about. What is not created in our minds as a consequence of how we talk about it doesn't exist for us. If you can't talk about something, then you cannot think about it. As we considered previously, our minds and how we talk about ourselves and our worlds are two aspects of the same thing.

To approach life as if it had a paper-and-pencil test (as is typical of most public schooling), with the answers at the back of the book, is no way to learn how to think. In fact, it is a way to learn how *not* to think. Many people approach life with the answers they have accumulated. The best way to approach life is with the imagination – with questions – as Einstein suggested. It's what you learn after you know it all that counts, as John Wooden insisted. What we take to be relevant is what the paper-and-pencil test may have on it. You can acquire "knowledge" and make it one of your possessions. But knowledge in and of itself doesn't do anything. Life requires performing life. And that begins and is carried by the kinds of questions one asks of herself and her world.

Henry Ford averred that "History is more or less bunk." And he continued:

> "...the only history that is worth a tinker's damn
> is the history we make today."

Life is in the future. There is no life in the past. The less you see your life in the future, the less life you have. There are many people who have no cause or purpose for their future. So they live diminishing lives. Robert Grudin, in his *Time and the Art of Living*, brought this perhaps painful perspective to bear:

> "...think of what you once wished or expected to
> have achieved by this point. Imagine what you will
> think of this period some time in the future. Will
> you think or do anything today that is worthy of
> future memory?"

That requires some thought. But it puts a point on Henry Ford's exclamation. What we think about today may not be worth a "tinker's damn." But if you architect and create in your world today something that is worthy of your future memory, your life will expand to fill your future in much the same way that not doing so will lead to a diminished, a sort of half-life. You show up in the future, but there was nothing for you to show up for. How you do or don't think about things today will always have consequences for your future life. To be unable to think leaves you with no recourse but to pursue entertaining or "fun" diversions today. We are always bartering the lives we have for the lives we could (or should) have. This requires being able to think what that path might be. Today you will be making the history of your life. Tomorrow you will be reflecting on it. To use Grudin's perspective, what is it that will make it worthy of future memory? And what is it that he means by "worthy"? Can having the answers that you assume preclude the thinking required of you be worthy? Why is it that we make choices about our lives from early on, but still they don't turn out the way we had hoped they would? And, as Grudin asks, will you make any choices today that will take you somewhere other than the way you wanted to go? Do you choose your work, or does your work choose you? Do you choose your life's companions or do they choose you?

+++++

Via our belief in the "self" over all, we have raised the individual (especially children) to the level of demigods. If there is not someone above you that you serve, then you are left to serving yourself. Princes and princesses for years (who were capably parented) were more deeply and widely educated for the lives they would live than were most others in their age groups. This was not a matter of affluence. It was a matter of discipline. What they learned was that only by respecting others could they gain the requisite self-respect. Those others were their carefully chosen mentors, whether modeled by their royal parents or having committed their wisdom in writing or tutoring. What Marines learn in boot camp is that only by respecting those higher than they are in the Corps would they have self-respect.

For the most part, it has been lost. Children who do not learn duty and responsibility as something higher than engaging in self-indulgence become demonic – either to those around them, or to themselves. A "tantrum" at any age is a reaction to a world that will not bend to one's will. If children are raised to have their own way, they will take it. If they can't have their own way, they lash out at those around them. We know that "road rage" is evidence of a failure to grow up. The Sioux did not raise their children to be demigods. Neither do Finnish parents. The Sioux Indians lasted for several thousand years. The Finns lived in the only country the Russians did not invade or conquer in WWII. There is something about discipline – especially discipline of mind and feelings – that is missing in our socialization. It is that people end up not having self-respect, because they never had to respect others.

The physicist Dennis Gabor (*not* a child psychologist) wrote in his 1964 book, *Inventing the Future*:

"The more permissive the society, the less permissive must be the education which makes the individual fit to live in it."

He was not referring to some prior epoch in which things were that way. His book was about the kind of future we are going to have if we keep going the direction we have been going. We live in perhaps the most permissive society that has ever existed. Our educational systems (and the parents involved) have not countered this drift by being less permissive. If anything, they have become more permissive over the years. So the paradox Gabor is writing about is not being handled either at school or at home and, even more recently, not at work either. We are raising a generation of spoiled kids who become spoiled adults who care about little else than their own pleasures. Judging from who volunteers for the military, few of our young people have much sense of duty or responsibility to the larger society. They seem to want their personal security and wellbeing, but they would prefer that there be a third-party payer (parents or government) for this. They are, in general, too busy playing with their games and other digital prostheses. We have ceased to consider the consequences of how we think about things, and what we do. We are a nation of privilege – of do what you want to do and let someone else pay for the consequences. Paradoxically, it is they who must eventually pay the price for their wantonness. Permissiveness means needing no conscience with respect to the consequences of just doing what one wants to do. If you want a 52" television screen, it should be provided by someone like the government. Do you need it? No. Is it going to improve the quality of your thinking or your life? Probably not.

So what makes us "fit" to live in our society is that we learn how to be addicted to being consumers (our GNP depends on it), and that we learn how to be indifferent to any of the consequences of our comportment, whether for ourselves or our society. The critical consequence is, of course, a perspective on life that may not be good either for the person or the society. It all begins and ends with how we think about things. If we can't, or prefer not to think about such critical factors as consequences, we are merely free to exploit our popular culture, and to be exploited by it. And we will be. We seek to abide by the current norms and fashions of our pop culture. We may be unhappy with the trajectory of our lives. But if that is the norm, so be it. We are more concerned with what we would lose if we changed our lives than what we might gain. We prefer the certainties of our familiar existence, even if those are more uncertain than we like to imagine. People adapt to the changing conditions of their lives because that is what most people do. They may complain about their lives, but put up with them because most people do. We are better at adapting to but still complaining about our lives, because that is what most people do. What "most people" do, or believe or think or feel, is more often than not taken as an imperative for all the rest of us. We smile when we are on camera. We laugh while drinking with others at the bar. We cry when something occurs that is considered a reason to do so by others. We use the facial expressions and the body "language" others seem to use in situations like the one we assume we're in. Eric Hoffer described it tersely as follows:

> *"When people are free to do as they please, they usually imitate each other."*

These sometimes become social movements. At other times, they are no more than the fashions of the day. When it becomes popular to "demonstrate" for or against something, there will always be people who are ready, willing, and able to do so. This may be because they have nothing better to do. It may be that they want to be where the action's at. Or it may be that they might be caught on camera, and being on television may be as close to immortality as they will ever be. Some people are attracted to these media events because such events seem more real to them (and more exciting) than their own mundane lives. If you are intrigued by how long people have been interested in this social phenomenon of imitation, try this metaphor from Juvenal (Roman poet of the late first-early second century A.D.)

> *"The grape gains its purple tinge by looking at another grape."*

In other words, people gain their ways of thinking by looking at how those in their social circles think about things. Since they cannot actually see the workings of the others' minds, they emulate the observable things, how those others make choices, how they dress and comport themselves in public, etc. They deduce how those other people think by what they *do* and how they do it. In the process, they begin to look like (and think like, as best they can) the people they are observing. Bees are more like bees than they are like owls because they look at the other bees. It's a very useful metaphor. Evan Esar offered a different perspective on this metaphor:

> *"Children are natural mimics who act like their parents in spite of every effort to teach them good manners."*

Emulating others that one knows can lead to good consequences or bad. What is exemplary is not always what is good. That's why the rational imposition of morality on people's behavior is so murky. If "everyone" is doing it, can it be wrong?

+++++

One's own mind – as wayward as they often are – may be inadequate for the task of plotting a life's course. But is it even possible that following the lead of what is popular or fashionable at the moment is necessarily a better beacon to navigate by? We don't normally chose people to be with who are committed to make us into better human beings. We are more likely to choose to be with them because they accept us the way we are – which is (tacitly) more like them. If "Wisdom is not communicable," as Siddhartha said, and if "You cannot confer a benefit on an unwilling (or incapable) person," as the Greeks understood, then how are people to learn from outside themselves what beacons they ought to be navigating their lives by? If people are not productively curious about how to live life, and with the best of the best thinkers' conclusions about this perennial conundrum easily and readily available, how are we to comprehend how their perspective on this keeps them on the purposeless paths they are on in their lives? Obviously not by trying to "teach" them. There is more wisdom available about how to live better lives than they might ever need. It can't be taught, but could be learned. And it is perhaps equally obvious that they are not going to learn how to live better lives by joining the thousands of fans at a celebrity concert or a highly-touted football game or at work. But then most people prefer a problem they can't solve to a solution they don't like. The solution may be that *they* have to change. And we all know how unlikely that is for most people. So disappointment reigns. But a whole industry has arisen to deal with the symptoms in one way or another. That may not be good for the people who are stuck, but it's good for the GNP.

There is a perspective on change which is shared by a few people. But the perspective on resistance to change seems to be shared by the multitudes. When people really get down to thinking about this – but if they can't, then there is no way to go but the way they are going. They may be knowledgeable. But knowing everything about everything does not make one capable of changing herself. There is no pill or cosmetic surgery for equipping one to do what has to be done to change one's life for the better. Besides, there is more social utility in complaining (along with others) about one's circumstances in life. *In any contest between the status quo and change, bet on the status quo.* If their lives are at stake, as we have seen previously, most people (95%) would rather die than change their familiar lifestyles. As Tolstoy famously remarked:

> "*Everyone thinks of changing the world, but no one thinks of changing himself.*"

But that would require the ability to think, which is in shrinking supply in our world. The corollary might be: "Most people may believe that someone ought to change the world to suit them, but rarely that they ought to change themselves in order to have that better world."

+++++

When trying to think about such things, and you can do it or you wouldn't be reading this book, it helps to remember this and to make it a part of your thinking:

> *Human minds and human communication are two aspects of the same thing. You can't engage in communication (either incoming or outgoing) without engaging your mind. And you can't engage your mind without at least talking to yourself (the most influential form of communication).*

It is with our own minds that we have to interpret *everything*. Our interpretations or explanations can be no better than our means of doing so – our own minds. You may be reading a book or magazine, or watching television, or chatting with a colleague. You may have carefully selected what to read, or watch, or chat about in advance (without being aware that you have done so) because you are vaguely aware of your own limits to understanding what is really going on. You also select on the basis of how well the encounter jibes with your perspective on things. Rarely do liberals attend a conservative lecture or conference – and vice versa. We want the values we believe in and depend upon to be confirmed, not to be challenged. We want *our* understanding to be *the* understanding we come away with. Coming out of such communication encounters, we want to be the same person we were going into it. We want our lexicons to be adequate to the task. We don't want to be provoked into growth. We want to be right, to take no significant risks in how we communicate, and with whom. We think with our limited minds for doing so. We don't want to be liberated from our ignorance or our stupidity. After all, we're who we are, and that's the important thing. We may be the "author" of whatever we read or watch or hear, because it is our interpretation that matters to us – simply because it is the truth. We may disagree with our interpretation of what we have heard or read. But that doesn't mean we disagree with the *source* of what we heard or read. Very few executives seem really to understand what Emerson said when he wrote:

"What you are thunders so that I cannot hear what you say to the contrary."

They seem to assume that they can be who they are but still be seen by their employees as they'd like to be seen (and heard). It just doesn't happen that way. Their employees (or their players if they are coaches) first "read" the person in order to come up with a way of interpreting the speaker. We have to "know" who is talking to us in order to create a paradigm for interpreting what they say. The mental image of them that we carry around with us determines how we interpret what others say. And our mental image of ourselves and of who we're talking to determines the kind of spin we put on what we say. We are essentially a different person when in communication with different people. What we say to person B about person C (not present) is not what we say to person C directly. And conversely. Undoubtedly this is what Shakespeare had in mind when he wrote *"All the world's a stage, /and all the men and women merely players...."* (He was of course playing the role of William Shakespeare, the playwright, when he wrote that. He was imagining who the audience would be, and how he would therefore have to spin his tale.) There is never a moment in your conscious life when you are not playing a role of one sort or another. How you think about what is going on always depends upon (a) what you imagine your role is in the story or vignette you imagine you're in, (b) how you imagine your role is to be played out, and (c) how capable *you* are of playing the role that you imagine is called for. You are the author of what you imagine to be the story and of how you script the role you play. Your world is comprised of the multitude of critics who judge your performance, and thus who you "are." You judge your performance. Either you are wrong, or "they" are. If you think of yourself as the ultimate judge, then the world is wrong. If you think of "them" as the ultimate judge, then you are wrong. We are forever suspended in those two forces.

We are who we "are" as a consequence of what we think about – and how we do so. What we think about is what we believe to be relevant to us. And then we take what is relevant to us to define us. Yet what we believe to be relevant to us may not be relevant in the circumstances in which we are called upon to play a role for which we may not be competent. Most of our psychological and social problems stem from the incompetence revealed in those situations. At work, we may take on a task for which we are not competent. The psychological damage may be significant. Or, socially, we may not know how to comport ourselves So we may not play the role well, and the whole episode sputters as a result. And our certainty about who we "are" is challenged. So we avoid those roles which do not confirm who we "are." It is those who choose the roles they can play well who seem to be the most successful in life. The rest of us channel our lives by hiding out in the roles we regularly perform. Our choices seem to be playing familiar roles over and over again or risking our identities in roles we didn't choose. And thus we come to believe that we have a "self" at our core. We don't. Ultimately, we can *be* no more than the roles which we are able to perform more or less adequately. The illusion of having a "self" comes from how we channel our lives in that direction.

+++++

We see the world and ourselves in it from the unique perspective of who we are, and how capable we are of going outside of the routine perspectives we have available. The more we use the same perspectives, the more habitual they become. The more habitual our thinking about things, given in how habitual it becomes, the more habitual *we* become.

Those who are lifelong learners become slightly different people than they were early on. And they become more potent – both for themselves and for the people who comprise the social circles to which they belong. As they grow, they grow into higher social circles. You cannot both grow in mental prowess and remain who you were. As William James advised:

> "Habit is...the enormous flywheel of society, its
> most precious conservative agent. It alone is what
> keeps us all within the bounds of ordinance."

The language is a bit antiquated. But what he means by "ordinance" is something like what is decreed or prescribed by our culture. Today we might refer to that as social control, and that our habits are at the core of social control. As our culture becomes more permissive, our society becomes less conservative and more turbulent here and there, as aided by the media. The media, as we have considered, focus on the exceptions, not on the rule. Thus, if you want to be a media celebrity, you have to break the rules. And the more "me"-centered (individualism) our society becomes, the less effective are the rules by which we are supposed to conduct our relationships in a civil society. We know that order breeds habit, and that disorder often breeds a heightened sense of being alive. Unless counteracted, the mind is a lazy thing. It prefers an orderly world, in which the algorithms it concocts often using no more than anecdotal cause-and-effect evidence. It does not readily distinguish causation from correlation. If it is poorly developed, it will produce poor results. Our habits are tacit. We are usually oblivious to our own. In *Pudd'nhead Wilson,* Mark Twain quipped:

> "Nothing so needs reforming than other people's habits."

Our perspectives, which if much used become habits – become ingrained. They become the framework for who we "are." We cling to our habits (usually unconsciously) as if our lives depended upon them. Perhaps our lives do depend on them. Certainly our sense of the continuity of our lives depends on transcendent habits. They are our devious way of "connecting the dots" of our lives. We might imagine we can outwit them. Usually we can't – we can't think them away. That's not how we got them. We are never so aware of our own habits as we are of others' habits – especially if others' habits are irritating to us. It is our own habits that get in the way, not theirs. Our own habits are the only ones we have the power to do something about. Others' habits are essentially givens in the context of what we are trying to accomplish. They can be changed, but only if you can make it necessary.

Habits always have practical consequences. For example, how you habitually carry out a phone call can be a waste of time. Or, when love becomes a habit, love ceases to exist. It was borne outside of any but the most personal small habits. In *Urn-Burial,* Sir Thomas Browne wrote:

"The long habit of living indisposeth us for dying."

Our habits are primarily for the routines of living. They are contrary to the habits that we might need to die well. The longer one is single, the more challenging will be coupling in everyday life. Our habits can impede our progress on what we want to accomplish and how we want to live. It is your perspective on your habits that controls your future.

+++++

If it weren't for adverse habits and for what we assume to be cultural (or fashionable) imperatives, we *could* choose what things mean to us. But perspectives are ingrained habits which we are rarely aware of. The measure of our lives lies in the consequences of how we think about things, and what we do about our thoughts. Life is measured by its consequences, not by its personal characteristics. A good life is good for the person who lives it, *and* for everyone who comes in contact with her or him. People commit suicide because they despair of being good for themselves or the world (internal and/or external) they think they inhabit.

The life we live is engendered in how we come to think about it and its imagined consequences. And underlying every thought is a perspective on what we are thinking about. Changing the perspective changes how we think about things. And how we think about things engenders the life we live day by day, year by year. The good life requires a New Year's Resolution, executed, every day. There are things to think about that are far more important than "fitting in." The first and the last of these are the consequences of your having lived at all. In *Money from Home,* Damon Runyon has his character say, *"I long ago [came] to the conclusion that all life is 6 to 5 against."* Isn't this all the more reason for strategic perspectives on what needs thinking about?

Perspective 6

How We Feel about Things

Most people want to feel good about themselves and the world they live in. That seems to happen only rarely and more or less randomly. We chase happiness and pleasure and camaraderie. We seem to be able to catch such feelings in a temporary but rarely in a permanent way. Is that because we don't understand what part of the problem *we* are? We tend to think that there is me, and there is the world outside of me, and that both are matters of fact. It is only when you come to the realization that neither is a matter of "fact" that you begin to see what part of any problem you face *you* are. It bears repeating: We do not see the world as it "is"…we see the world as *we* are. That's the base underlying perspective we need to internalize. The world we "see" and who we are, are two aspects of the same thing. There is no world to be seen apart from an "I" looking at it. And then it will be seen as that "I" sees it.

No human is born knowing all of the answers. No human is born knowing even what questions to ask. No human is born capable of having *comprehensible* feelings. The feelings we are aware of having are the ones we have as a consequence of who we *are*. The feelings we have depend upon the flavor of the kool-aid we have drunk along the way. How did the person who got the first injection by needle know it was supposed to hurt, or at least to have feelings of apprehension about it? How did the first person who ever "fell" in love know what feelings were supposed to come with it? If you and no one you know had ever heard of "love," would you still have the same feelings about it? When you die, you no longer have the human feelings that you had when you were alive. Where do they go? Where did they come from in the first place? Did you decide what feelings you wanted to have in your life before you were born? Animals in the wild may or not have "feelings." How would we know? They don't talk about them. Nor do they display them in public. We can anthropomorphize. But the feelings we would attribute to them are not the feelings some culture closer to them would attribute to them. Our culture is full of explanations about what feelings are appropriate in what circumstances, and how they are to be performed in public. We know, as Eleanor Roosevelt said, that no one can make you feel bad without your permission. We seem to be following normative protocols about feelings and their expression. That means they must be socially prescribed and proscribed. We know that people who express fear are easier targets for criminals than are people who do not perform fear in their presence. It takes some training away from the popular culture, but the Samurai learned to be fear-less, and thus actually had to fight fewer actual battles, an insight not lost in the training today for the Special Forces. A perspective in which you do not fear death makes it *less* likely that you will have to do so at the hands of your adversary. Fear in a boxing ring makes you more vulnerable to your opponent, as it does in poker.

The issue, of course, is what things mean to you, given the culture and the subcultures in which you have learned how to have feelings by expressing them. If happiness, for example, is something that happens to you from outside yourself, you have one perspective. If it is your obligation to your social circle/community to be happy (as it was for many American Indian cultures), you have a very different perspective. In the one, you wait for happy things to happen to you, and you may feel left out if they don't. In the other, you express happiness as a cultural mandate, and by expressing happiness, you have it, you feel it. So the first thing you need to know about feelings is just this:

You don't have feelings and then express them. As
a general rule, you have certain feelings when, and
IF, you express them.

In our culture, this is counter-intuitive. We are taught to believe that feelings are something that happens to us. We are taught to believe that both our feelings and our expression of them is just a part of human nature. But what we refer to as "human nature" varies (sometimes greatly) from culture to culture, and often from subculture to subculture. Pain, for example, is very culture specific. In some cultures, expressing pain is a sign of character weakness. We are encouraged in our own culture to express pain – in large or small ways. It is not that one culture is right and therefore that other cultures are wrong. They are different because they are different. They emerged in different circumstances and evolved over time as their beliefs and perspectives took the direction they took. Things are the way they are because they got to be that way. And cultures are not self-correcting. They continue on in the direction they are going. Cultures are basically teleological – which means that they grow out of the way they are, not the way they ought to be. After Napoleon, France was pretty much what it was before Napoleon. As Stanislaw Lec put it, metaphorically:

> *"In an avalanche, no individual snowflake feels*
> *responsible."*

Social evolution is like an avalanche that moves on according to the way it is, seemingly until exhausted. It is the people who comprise the society who *are* responsible. But few of those people "feel" responsible for the direction the society is moving. "Is" trumps "ought to be" almost every time – both individually and collectively. Gustave Le Bon offered this perspective on the strength of emotions over rationality:

> *"One feeling may be opposed by another feeling,*
> *but never by reason."*

Decisions and actions arrived at irrationally (by the emotions attendant to the perspectives we live by) cannot be negated or disrupted by a rational argument. Our feelings take precedence – again both individually and collectively. What's right is what we *feel* is right. We often know the right thing to do. But, if history is any guide, we seldom do the right thing. Feelings trump intellect most of the time. It requires more willpower to overcome the feelings that most people have about things that matter to them. It is pointless to tell the mother of a newborn that her baby is "ugly." After the anticipation and travail of nine months, that can simply not be so.

+++++

The first dilemma that needs to be sorted out in order to gain a sound perspective on how we feel about things is this:

> *What makes all the difference is whether or not*
> *you have chosen the feelings that you have, or they*
> *have chosen you.*

This may require some reflection on your part, and here some mindful exploration. In our culture, the possibility that one can chose one's operant feelings is rarely considered. We are led to believe that our feelings are something that just happens to us, with no intention on our part. Given how variously feelings are conceived of in different cultures, it seems clear that feelings are *socially* constructed, enacted, felt, and expressed. There may be a couple of exceptions at birth. But once the child becomes verbal (capable of participating in social- and self-communication), the psychic and social byproducts are literally all socially constructed and maintained in our dialogues with others and ourselves. In the context of the range of social possibilities or individual invention, a person could actually choose the feelings that he or she imagines might be what's needed to further their cause in life. But in our culture, we are supposed to be the victims of the feelings that take us not where *we* want to go, but where *they* take us. "I just don't feel like it" is the excuse for many situations. But what we know is that competent people do what needs to be done whether they "feel" like it or not. People who are not as competent typically opt out by expressing that they don't "feel" like doing what needs to be done. Competent people bet on themselves. Less than fully competent people bet on the circumstances, of which they see themselves as the victim. Could you *choose* the feelings you want or need? Yes, apparently so. Lincoln once remarked: *"Most folks are as happy as they make up their minds to be."* It's not a case of mind over matter. It's a case of making your feelings work for you rather than you working for your feelings. Being victimized by our feelings is simply a matter of the pervasive influence of the pop culture.

Another challenge to our pop psych perspective on feelings as the dominant perspective comes from Thomas Carlyle in his well-known book, *On Heroes, Hero-Worship, and the Heroic in History:*

> *"The thoughts they had were the parents of the actions they did; their feelings were the parents of their thoughts."*

It's likely that no more than a few moderns have ever considered that sequence. We think of our feelings as being triggered by outside forces, and our reactions as being natural, even obligatory. But what Carlyle, who spent years researching such things, asserted was that it is our feelings that drive our thoughts, and not the other way around. We think of feelings as being the result of what happens, not the cause of what we think and thus what we do. In James Miller's *Word, Self, Reality,* we come face to face with another challenge to our pop cultural perspective:

> *"To know what we think, we must know how we feel. It is feeling that shapes belief and forms opinion. It is feeling that directs the strategy of argument."*

Beyond so nicely confirming Carlyle's conclusions (but from a very different perspective), Miller's last sentence is very provocative for our purposes. He writes that "It is feeling that directs the strategy of argument." Strategy here refers to how a person views himself or his world when it is different from what he or she has expected or hoped for. In other words, if there is a discrepancy between what was anticipated and what actually happens, the person has an "argument" to resolve. This might also be thought of as a problem to be solved. What that implies is that feelings arise in all such discrepancies between what is expected and what appears to be the reality of the situation. One's mind is a hypothetical or conjectural thing. It is forever making theories about how things work and about how we are to fit into any conceptualization of the world beyond that involves us. If things work out the way we expect them to (given our perspectives on the present or the future), no argument with ourselves or others. If they don't work out according to our expectations, we have an "argument" with ourselves about whether we were wrong or other people are wrong. How that challenge to our minding of the world works out bears upon our identity in the world we inhabit. It is not a trivial matter. Who we *are* is at stake. People are confirmed or disconfirmed in such conflicts of perspective. The consequences make us who we "are." For example, if your spouse or partner turns out to have been "cheating" on you for some time, your argument with yourself begins with something like, "I can't believe it." In coming to terms with the facts of the matter, you resolve in some way the differing perspectives. If you can't resolve the discrepancy between what you expected and what actually happened, then you will agonize over your failure to reconcile the two perspectives. If it rains on your picnic, you can take it personally, or as just one of those things that happen – like "falling" in love, or falling ill. We can't control what happens. But we have full control over how we interpret it. However we do so, it will resolve the argument we are having with ourselves – for better *or* for worse.

A. R. Ammons provides a useful perspective on this:

> *"I attended the burial of all my rosy feelings:*
> *I performed the rites, simple and decisive."*

For most people, such burial rites are neither simple nor decisive. But, he is intimating, they could be. When we bury our rosy feelings about someone or something, we are burying a part of ourselves. We are far better off to do so simply and decisively. Ask anyone who has lost a spouse or a child. In *Stories. The Angel of the Bridge* (1978), John Cheever wrote:

> *"It was at the highest point in the arc of a bridge*
> *that I became aware suddenly of the depth and the*
> *bitterness of my feelings about modern life, and of*
> *the profoundness of my yearning for a more vivid,*
> *simple, and peaceable world."*

Sometimes these discrepancies between the world we inhabit and the yearning for a better world lead us into a deep and bitter set of feelings about our lives in our worlds. We can be reasonably certain that those who suffer the pangs of war or disaster have deep feelings about what is happening, or what happened, to them. If they have seen pictures or read stories about how people express their feelings about such awful happenings, they have recipes for expressing their anguish. We may seem to be helpless in the situation, but we have some recipes for how we would argue with ourselves or express our feeling to others. In this sense, feelings are contagious. By expressing their feelings, people provide other people with recipes for how they are supposed to feel if this or that happens. In expressing their feelings, those other people actually *have* the feelings they are expressing. It may be that the despair Cheever is expressing comes from his inability to reconcile the world as he would have it and the world that he lives in. The world will not change just because he (or any one of us, for that matter) is bitter about modern life. He can't change "modern life." No individual can. So what is the point to being bitter about it?

"All violent feelings…produce in us a falseness in
all our impressions of external things…."

This is how John Ruskin put it to us in *Modern Painters, III* (1856). Perhaps he didn't put it as well as he might have. But we know what he meant – which is that when your feelings are running high (or deep) you see the world outside of us more falsely than usual. When you feel that you are wildly and irreversibly in love, for example, the most rational perspectives you may be offered will be rejected. When you are feeling deeply in grief you are not likely to be moved by the conventional bromides offered by those around you. Our clear-sightedness betrays us when we are deeply or widely into our own feelings. So what do we want all of this to mean to us about how we *feel* about things?

Mainly this: feelings have consequences inevitably and mainly for the person who performs them. If they are strong feelings, the consequences will be more potent. If they are trivial, the consequences are likely to be trivial. The closer they are to who we *are*, the more likely they are to be profoundly consequential for who we become. When our feelings run deep (with or without justification), the consequences are more likely to be disruptive of our lives. The more disruptive those consequences, the more staying power they will have. This may account for more suicides and more destructive behavior than we might see through our pop-cultural lenses. Beliefs begin and end with feelings.

The other lesson is this one. Our feelings emerge in some discrepancy between what we want or expect to happen and what is actually happening. If we had no expectations, we would be unlikely to have any feelings one way or the other. This is why some people are unperturbed by what happens in their worlds – inner or outer. If they don't care much what happens, their feelings about themselves and their lives will be lukewarm. If you are immune to being frustrated, you're not likely to have strong feelings. If the lover you don't really like dumps you, you may feel more freedom than impediments in your life. We can be glad for the wrong reasons, or we can be sad for the right reasons. Either way, we may have some feelings about the situation, and those feelings will have consequences for us, but not much for other people.

Our feelings are always subjective, and their consequences – in our thoughts and actions – will also be subjective.

Our perspective on our feelings, where they come from, and where they lead us, is central to how we live our lives and who we become as a result. They can be sources for our good or our ill. If we don't manage them, they will manage us.

+++++

If you dream upon a star, in our culture, your dreams may come true. Well, they mostly didn't, and won't. The only dreams that come true are anomalies. They are the exceptions, driven by uncontrolled coincidences. This doesn't mean that if you work your butt off you will be "successful." Success comes in a multitude of forms. It depends upon how you *feel* about your present life. Some people feel despondent when they have everything. Other people feel fine when they have nothing. It all depends on the interpretations you impose on your circumstances. In Sister Carrie, Theodore Dreiser proffered this thought:

> *"In your rocking chair by your window shall you
> dream such happiness as you may never feel."*

As probably intended, this provokes an interesting perspective on the whole business of feelings that we may not always be aware of. And that is that most people live in two worlds more or less simultaneously: one of those worlds is a person's inner thoughts and feelings – which are private and only judiciously made public. The other world is the world tempered by the reality outside oneself, the world of what people think of that person, and what their feelings are about him or her. (A third world of course is the "objective" world of what is said to be happening beyond anyone's intentions or control, like the weather.

We may have feelings about this world, but it cannot have feelings about us, one way or the other.) Your feelings about yourself, your perspectives on yourself, are not the same as the perspectives other people harbor of you.

There are three ways of making your dreams come true:

- One is to *live* in your dreams as if they were real.
- Another is to pursue them in your dreams.
- The third is to pursue them in the social and socially artifactual world you inhabit, where thousands of others are pursuing theirs.

Your feelings will take you in one of these three ways. In the first, you are living a delusion in a real world (which may make you happy or sad, healthy or unhealthy in mind and thus in spirit). The second requires you to sit in your rocking chair and fantasize, based on the assumption that's all there is. The third requires you to enter into a contest with the people and the social institutions in place, in order to mold that world to suit you. Radical leaders have tried to do this from the beginning of human societies on this earth. Is the world you inhabit there to satisfy you, or to fulfill itself? We can dream better lives than we can engineer for ourselves. It is in the discrepancy between the two that our feelings about ourselves and the world we inhabit (as interpreted by us) arise. The consequences are in the imagined conflict between the two. Whose agenda will be fulfilled – yours or that of your world?

It comes down to a conflict about how the future is made. There are the forces of people's will (or the dreams to which they are addicted).

And then there are the forces of social evolution, which are largely independent of our wishes. We are the snowflake in the avalanche (as Lec put it). Can we reverse it? Can we redirect it? Can any one person bend it to their will? That hasn't happened in history. The only thing any one of us controls is how we feel about things, which gives rise to how we think about things. As long as we assume that feelings are a result of what happens to us, the forces of social evolution will always win. If we believe that we (in large numbers) can actually choose our feelings about things, and thus how we think about things, those forces may be the ones in command – individually and collectively. Even if that happened (which is highly unlikely) we would still have to contend with the agendas (the feelings) of others in our worlds. There has always been this conflict between the person and his or her society. We can rewrite our pasts. It's our futures that are at stake. And that's what drives our present feeling, thinking, being, and doing. Who do you intend to be? In which world do you intend to realize yourself?

People have differing *tastes*. If they are about cars or home decoration or the clothes they wear, the consequences are largely how in-fashion or out of fashion they appear to others. But our tastes in spouses, or in choosing our influencers or lifestyles or nutrition, can have serious long-lasting consequences. Tastes are not the same as feelings. They, like our other perspectives, are driven by feelings. However they can take us in the direction of "morality" – which has to do with the consequences of our feelings, both for us as individuals and the society in which we live our lives. Just because you have a taste for this or that doesn't make it efficacious for you – or for the rest of your world. Just because everybody you know and like has similar tastes does not make those tastes efficacious for any of the people who share them – or for the society in which you indulge your tastes. Like your opinions, your tastes are not "right" just because you are the one who espouses them. Our tastes are a manifestation of our perspectives on ourselves and our worlds. And, just like our opinions, they have consequences – for us particularly and for the world in which we exercise our narcissisms. Oscar Wilde is known for his contrarian witticisms. His provocation here is as follows:

> *"Good taste is the excuse I've always given for leading such a bad life."*

He did often blatantly violate the customs of his day. But there are many people who claim to have a "bad life" – or at least a life that is less than the one they dream of. Their "bad life" did not originate in good taste as an excuse. There are multifarious ways of having a bad life, and more are being invented every day. Wilde was very articulate, which made him an enemy of the people who do not see articulateness as a path to any life they might choose. He was flamboyant. He wanted his life to be seen as the story of his life, not just picayune contrariness.

He paid dearly for his tastes. Seemingly the only way to escape such social punishment is to stick closely to the norms and fashions of the day. If you don't stand out, you can't be singled out for social retribution. Those who speak out (in words or dress) against the conventional ways of feeling and doing in any culture will pay the price. Liberators are acceptable only to those people who are passionate about being liberated. Many of the nay-sayers about women's "liberation" were women. They saw the movement as going from one form of oppression to another, since they would be expected to conform to the protocols and perspectives of the movement rather than the ones they had adapted to. As the old adage has it, "One person's tastes are another person's poison." It's unlikely that you would ever see a fashion model in an all-you-can-eat fast food place. We go where our tastes go, unless we defy them for reasons having to do with how we want to be seen by others. As the columnist Evan Esar quipped:

> "The self-admiration of some people proves that
> there's no accounting for taste."

And no accounting, as well, for the *feelings* that produce and justify those tastes.

+++++

What we "understand" when we understand something we have heard or read is our understanding of our *interpretation* of what we have heard or read. When we don't understand something we have heard or read, it's because we can't come up with an interpretation that makes sense to us personally. Unless, of course, we are being intentionally devious, in which case our understanding or not understanding is a ploy serving our own agenda in the matter. We do this dozens or hundreds of times every day. It is a characteristic of being a modern human. Our worlds are overfilled with information about every subject known to mankind. Do we understand everything that is going on? No. Would we want to, or need to, understand everything that is channeled our way?

No. So what does our everyday understandings and misunderstanding have to do with our *feelings* about things?

We generally *feel* like we understand what it is we are capable of understanding, and *feel* like we don't understand anything that conflicts with what we already understand. We are more or less "open" to confirmation of what we already understand, and more or less "closed" to what we do not understand. New understandings come to us only if we feel like they serve our purposes – and only if they don't require us to change our perspective of ourselves or our worlds in any significant way.

This is usually very tacit, and we are not usually aware of how or why we choose to understand what we understand, and why we don't understand what we don't understand. This is at the heart of who we are, of who we associate with, what our feelings are about the influences that whirl around us, or even what our feelings have to do with anything.

We've encountered this previously. But it bears repeating. If someone says to you, "I love you," you will understand what that means if you feel the same way and want to move on. If someone says to you, "I love you," and you want nothing to do with that person, you won't understand what the other person has said. If you are a mathematician, it will behoove you to understand what another mathematician is saying. If you are not, you will feel okay about not understanding any of it. If you are not a skeptic about what is happening in your world, you will feel you have no need to understand any of it. If you are a skeptic, you will understand what skeptics are saying about what is happening in your world, or about certain controversial ideas. If you are a scientist, you will understand what scientists say about things. If you are not, you may feel like you have no interest in that conversation. We have a perspective on what we hear or read, which emanates who we are. That perspective predicts to whether or not we will understand or not understand what we hear or read. Our feelings are, ultimately, what we feel might be useful to us in some social or occupational way.

What is most interesting about this matter of "understanding" is given in this small scenario: If someone says to you, "I love you," you will likely say "I love you too" – IF indeed you want to take the path most taken. But, note carefully, you don't know what that person means by what they say – that is, you don't really understand. But let's say that you take the conventional path where one thing leads to another in a fairly predictable way. Then one day that person says, "I don't love you any more." You will have trouble and some anguish trying to "understand" that. We believe that understanding something (or someone) enables us to control that something – or that someone. The truth of the matter is that the person who started the whole thing didn't really know what he or she meant by what they said. Your understanding was a matter of understanding your interpretation of what they said. We can "know" what people need even if they haven't a clue themselves. It's a psychosocial (communication) game from which no one ever can escape.

You assume you know what was meant by what you heard or read or observed. But the best you can do is to understand your own interpretation – or not. You assume that others will understand what you meant by what you said to them. There are two problems with this assumption: one is that you may not know what *you* meant by what you said (or did). The old saying is: "How do I know what I mean until I've heard what I said?" In other words, it is your interpretation of what you said that you understand. And for those others, it is their interpretation of what you said (or did) which they "understand." A competent reader will try to understand what an author meant by what that author wrote or said. A competent listener will try to understand what a person meant by what they said (or did). But the interpretation can never be any better than the interpreter is as a listener or a reader. We can equip ourselves to be better at it. But we can never eliminate the interpretation at either end.

A speaker or writer will never be any better at saying what they mean than he or she is capable of. A listener or reader will never be any better at that task than he or she is capable of. Understanding is not a function of the communiqué. It is a function of the person who is performing as the origin or the destination of that communiqué – whether that is a conversation, a happening or a scene, or a book or a talk or TV. Photos do not function unfiltered. They exist only in their interpretations by the photographers who produced them and the people who consume them. There is no way of talking about something unfiltered by the talker. There is no way of reading about something unfiltered by the reader. We are who we are by virtue of how we filter what we "understand." As Henri Amiel wrote in his Journal of 7 April, 1866:

> *"We only understand that which is already within us."*

We must necessarily interpret what we see and hear. Others must necessarily interpret what we say and do. There is no escaping that. We don't talk about "the" world. We talk about our interpretation of it. Others are not capable of understanding "the" world, but only their interpretation of it. What things mean comes back to our understanding of what things mean…to us. Between you and the world you observe, there is always your interpretation of it. Between you and other people, there is always their interpretation of what you say and do.

Understanding is always subjective. There is no "objective" understanding. How we *feel* about things is already underwriting our interpretations. We live by what is already within us – by what is already who we *are*. We see the world not as it is, but as we are. We feel about things not as *they* are, but as *we* are.

> *"Some people understand nothing better than anything else."*
>
> --Evan Esar

Perspective 7

Words, Numbers, Measures, & Logic

Cave art and sand art were examples of ancient ways of representing our worlds and our environments to ourselves. It was one thing to apprehend nature directly. But humans have always seemed to have a need to represent themselves and the creatures and the happenings of their environments in one form or another. When people began to wonder where they came from, they composed creation stories – stories that told where they came from and how they happen to have the conscious lives they had. Every culture until recently had a quite unique creation story. The inhabitants of ancient India had an elaborate and extensive creation story, as did the Aborigene of Australia, whose oral stories of creation and how to live was memorized by all and sung while they were on their "walkabouts." American Indian tribes had similar but distinctive creation stories of their own. Those, along with rules of conduct, became an indispensable method of socializing newcomers into the culture. The need, seemingly, was (and remains) that of rendering our human existence in some form that transcended our short lives and provided some small measure of objectivity. We began to know who we were by the stories we told and the drawings that represented and thus explained how human life was to be thought of. The various forms of representing us by some method or other became the fulcrum on which we created our pasts, our present, and our futures. Without those means of representing ourselves to ourselves, we would have remained the quasi-mute animals that we were initially. We explained ourselves and our worlds to the generations that succeeded us.

All of the forms of explaining ourselves to ourselves began when we began to be human. That's what it means to be human – to be mindful of who we are individually and collectively, and to comport ourselves as we are culturally supposed to comport ourselves. We are not hard-wired for such things like other animals. We had to create ourselves and our unique ways of doing things. Representing ourselves by some method was the beginning. We created thereby a virtual reality that previously was our only reality. We lifted ourselves out of the darkness and into the light by talking about ourselves and our worlds in different ways. In our talk, we represented ourselves as distinctly human in the early stages of mindfulness and even more critical, self-mindfulness. Our minds arose in those struggles to be mindful of ourselves. We sang, we danced, we painted and sketched ourselves, we sat or walked together telling our stories of our uniqueness and our destinies. We honored our beginnings and invented ways of explaining everything that we wondered about.

People knew that life was fleeting. So they sought some modicum of immortality in how they depicted their lives in singing or dancing about them, and in their more permanent representations of them. By making more permanent representations of their lives, they gave their lives that modicum of immortality. They passed on to succeeding generations the ways in which we came to see and think of ourselves in our worlds. Our ways of immortalizing ourselves may be infinitely more sophisticated, but they function in much the same way. The primary function is to socialize ourselves and our progeny. We are refracted in how we represent ourselves to ourselves and to others in our social groups. In representing ourselves in some social way, we created ourselves. We exist in how we are thus triangulated into a social group, tribe, or clan. It is the unique culture in which we live that is our Mother. We are made sentient there by our inherited and invented explanations and representations and depictions of ourselves.

Any way of explaining ourselves and our worlds is of course a *perspective* on our worlds and ourselves in them. To attend a celebration in ancient times helped to create those cultural perspectives. To memorize the music or the lyrics of contemporary tunes in our time is a source of our perspectives – as are schooling, occupational groups, TV series, epistemic communities, social circles and the socialization that goes on via commercial advertising. Most American workers know what is meant by "It's Miller Time!" It's a way of demarking the conceptual and affective difference between the pleasures of leisure time and the displeasures of working at a "job." We "get to" go to the movies or the rock concert. We "have to" go to work or do our homework. Words repeated become the tags for concepts of increasing complexity or rigid inflexibility. They are our pop culture. They become the highways of our lives. Our lexicons are not just our vocabularies – the words we use most frequently. They are the toolboxes of our minds. What we can't talk about, we can't experience. When we can't understand, we may just pretend by being agreeable or sympathetic.

+++++

Over time, every human endeavor is aided by technology. To explore the ocean floor personally requires you to wear a high-tech body suit and breathing equipment, along with a wrist-worn gadget that measures the depth you are at. In every culture, the application of *numbers* spurred its evolution. Before numbers, there were words. Before words, there were various forms of pictographs. They contributed to civilization. And our technologies were and are at the core of our evolution as societies and of our everyday lives as humans in those evolving societies. It's difficult to imagine an existence without numbers, for example. You have to understand numbers to dial a telephone, or to set your clock. The dashboard in your car wouldn't make much sense to you if you didn't understand numbers and measures. Measurements of all sorts depend upon the prior invention of numbers. When you learn to cook in the modern world, you learn by the numbers. Some even think that you can learn to paint "by the numbers." They are as essential to our lives in the modern world as are breathing or commuting. Not so long ago, if you wanted food, you had to provide it for yourself. Now you go to the supermarket where every product is described by numbers – if not in terms of their nutritional value, then in terms of price, which after all consists of numbers.

+++++

If you don't know what a person means when they call another person a "10," it's either because you didn't grow up in America, or you didn't see the movie. Our proverbs, and many of our clichés, are the sediment of our cultural wisdom, coming into popular use because "everyone else" uses them (usually in lieu of thinking). For example, "The early bird gets the worm." What does that mean, pragmatically? Ben Franklin assumed it meant something like "Early to bed, early to rise." Proverbs are usually tacit lessons about how to live. They offer a perspective on the multifarious aspects of everyday life, and they are found in every known human culture. For example:

- *Love is a sweet dream, and marriage is the alarm clock* (Jewish).
- *Tears are a language, but only he who weeps understands them* (Armenian).
- *It is a lonely washing that has no man's shirt in it* (Irish).
- *One of the greatest labor-saving inventions of today is tomorrow* (American).
- *'Tis a bad house that has not an old man in it* (Italian).
- *At digging time only one man will turn up; at harvest time there is no limit to the number of helpers* (Maori).

Newcomers to a culture are not socialized properly until they can readily interpret these metaphors. All language is metaphoric. But explicating these kernels of folk wisdom is everywhere a sign of successful socialization. There is often something ironic in them, and many are a bit humorous – because what we can laugh at is what we learn best. Consider the Irish proverb for a moment. What does it mean? And what are its implications for living an Irish life? To a properly socialized Irish person, it means that the best life is one shared with someone of the opposite sex. It means that there is a kind of traditional division of labor, and that the absence of one or the other makes for a sad perspective. It may also be taken to mean that caring about the other is how well you carry out your domestic responsibilities.

Can such trivial sayings have profound consequences? Indeed they can. From the many proverbs that are heard and taught, a person gains a unique cultural perspective on the world and himself or herself in it. Love is not lifelong romance. It comes down to how competent one is at the everyday chores that belong to him or her. The Irish in general have had far fewer problems with "love" than we have in America. That's because we grow up with different perspectives on love and marriage than other cultures have. Do words make a difference in how we see the world? We see our worlds and ourselves in them according to the perspectives (the concepts) with which we observe and understand them. If you want to know how someone raised in another culture views the world, listen to the clichés they use to talk. If you want to know how someone socialized into an epistemic community different from yours, listen to the clichés they use to describe the ways of the world in which they live. Those who are socialized into the ways of the Mafia will have a quite different perspective on the world than does someone socialized as a farmer, or as a part of a royal family. Anyone socialized in another culture (not yet Westernized) has a different perspective on how to live their lives. We socialize our children somewhat differently than any other culture. The cultural values are implicit in how we explain and talk about things. This requires words or numbers or images.

Franz Kafka remarked, *"The true word leads; the untrue misleads."* The "true" word is not so much the word that clearly identifies something in the real word. It is more so the word that is efficacious – the word that bodes well for the future of the speaker and the listener. There are no neutral words. They either contribute to the life we have chosen, or they lead us down the wrong path for the life we have chosen. In a speech in London in February,1923, Rudyard Kipling said:

> *"Words are ... the most powerful drug used by mankind."*

It's a metaphor worth thinking about. Words may sharpen or dull our wits in the short term, just as other drugs do. But in the long term they have consequences that we may or may not be aware of, but affect us for good or ill nonetheless. Talking has consequences. Listening – any kind of paying attention to something or someone – has consequences. As a technology of communication, words can lead us to wonderful things, some of which came from Kipling. Freud (after Milton) wrote that the words we use in everyday communication with one another can lead us to our heavens or our hells. Words are the tags for the meaning of things. And the meanings we attribute to things are provided by every individual mind, are thus become the pathways of our lives. They can take us where we ought to go. But they can also take us where we ought not to go, just as our drugs can. Why the most "powerful" drug used by mankind? Two reasons: one is that we are the most careless with them, the main infrastructure of our individual and collectives lives. We are inadequately disciplined in our use of them. The other reason is that they have far more extended consequences. They alter our perspectives on ourselves and our worlds in the most fundamental way. Words – powerful drugs – in the minds of careless people is a recipe for either enriching one's life … or for damaging it in some way.

But we exercise a prerequisite when we talk to or listen to other people, either directly or via the media. It is that who we interpret them to BE is the basis for interpreting their words. In one of his famous letters to his son, Lord Chesterfield in 1973 wrote:

> *"Mind not only what people say, but how they say it; and if you have any sagacity, you may discover more truth by your eyes than by your ears. People can say what they will, but they cannot look just as they will; and their looks frequently [reveal] what their words are calculated to conceal."*

Most people know this, because they have had conversations with salespeople and politicians and friends who wanted something from them but expressed it as if it were to benefit them. The operant term

here is "sagacity." He is saying to his son, "…if you have any sagacity…."
Sagacity is an interesting word – it implies keen mental discernment and
good judgment, maybe even shrewdness. Most people never gain these
qualities, so they are victims of the catchwords of the day, like "Save!"
money by buying something you don't need just because it is on sale.
Politicians make campaign promises. It's usually just talk.

So words can conceal as well as they can reveal. If you can inform or
incite by words, you can deceive by words. They mean what they mean
to the person on whom they land by eye or ear, whether intentional
or not.

People talk. There is often no reliable correlation between what
people say and what those same people do. Your interpretation is your
interpretation. What a word or a batch of words mean is a function
of the interpreter, not the words. When someone yells "FIRE!!" in
the building, you may take escape action. But the speaker may only
have been curious about what you would do. There was no fire. That's
what makes life interesting: you live by your perspectives and your
interpretations, not by any "reality." A "reality" TV show is produced
by people. It is only the creators' perspective, and its intent is not to
improve your life, but theirs. So they will put on the screen whatever
you are willing to pay for by consuming the fare of the commercial
investors. A person may say they "love" you. But you can't know what
conniving they are up to. If you need the expression, they will provide
it, whether by body or by words. You will "read" them to decide what
you think your interpretation should be. But if they're even reasonably
cunning, they can provide you with what you're willing to pay for – in
some form. In a commercial culture such as ours, there are predators
and there is their prey. You will either influence or be influenced.
Politicians are predators – in or out of bureaucratic organizations – as
are car dealers, retailers, teachers, preachers, experts, doctors, lawyers,
artists and art dealers, and often social acquaintances. Everybody
wants something from everybody else, and that is always their hidden
agenda. They may cast it as if it were to benefit you (as in "SALE!!"),
but if they weren't benefitting more, they wouldn't be bothering you.
Beauty is inherited and then packaged. If you've got it, you can benefit

yourself by exploiting it. If you haven't, clever marketers will exploit you through your attempts to get something you don't have and thus envy. A word is a way of gaining a perspective on anything and everything people want to think about or do something about. They were once pictographs. Given our technologies, our photographs and videos and other publically-shared representations function the same way. They are the building blocks of mental concepts – and/or of hypotheses about anything and everything people want to think about or do something about. They become the virtual reality we inhabit in our minding of our worlds.

When words and images are combined in a popular and clever way, together they can be almost irresistible. You are lured into buying the sizzle, whether in love or steak dinners. But what you get is what you get. We go through the motions of our cultural and individual algorithms.

But what we get is what we get. Different perspectives lead to different outcomes.

+++++

Numbers are intriguing. They are a wholly human-invented and continuously-evolving perspective on the world. Numbers may be useful. But they change forever our perspective on certain things. How could there ever be a competitive sport like football without numbers? Even the old-fashioned game of "Marbles" played by youngsters was by-the-numbers. Bras are categorized by numbers, as are shoes and shirts. There would be no opticians without numbers. We count the number of children we have, and we count our money. We count the number of people in the country, and we count the votes. We know most of the things in our lives by the numbers. It is perhaps possible that people have always counted certain things, on their fingers or by an abacus or other device. We count the days before…and we count the days after…. Can you imagine an employment report from the government, or news about an oncoming hurricane, without numbers? Can you imagine "telling" time in the modern world without numbers? Would the world we know even be possible without numbers?

Like words, we take our numbers for granted. We think with them. We anticipate and justify what happens by them. Harold Geneen (in his book *Managing)* described this to us as follows:

> *"When you have mastered the numbers, you will*
> *in fact no longer be reading numbers, any more*
> *than you read words when reading a book. You*
> *will be reading meanings."*

We *experience* the story we are reading when we read a book. In the same way, we experience the world according to the numbers that are used to explain it. Numbers create a unique perspective on things. Chefs know how much a "pinch" of salt in their preparations means. Novices may read a recipe that calls for a half-teaspoon of salt, and buy or use a spoon that holds just that much salt. Houses are built by the numbers, just as skyscrapers are. If there are no gas stations along your route, it pays to know how much gasoline you have in your vehicles tank, and how much gasoline it guzzles per mile of your commute. With all that counting, you would think that no one would ever run out of gas. But they do. When trekking up a glacier, it may help to know roughly how far across the crevasse is, in order to bring a ladder which is longer than the crevasse is wide. When buying a hat or a shirt by the numbers, it may help to know what "size" to buy. A tape measure has numbers on it. So does a ruler. So does the laser that counts the feet or inches for you. The thousands of planes that crisscross the skies regularly are following a designated highway. Those highways in the sky are calculated by numbers. Your age is determined by numbers, just as the days and months and the hours and the minutes are.

The Italian theater director and actor Fulvio Fiori once remarked:

> *"Numbers are the only thing mathematicians can*
> *count on."*

That is more than cleverly obvious. We have come to live in a world where numbers are the infrastructure for most of our cultural artifacts.

Words are evolutionary. They open up worlds that could never be thought of before. Numbers are evolutionary, in the sense that they make possible the tangible artifacts that underlie and characterize our social and material environments – like jet planes, self navigating vehicles, cheap clothing, and ready food supplies, schools, and computers. There is not much that is not calculated by the numbers. We do "number-crunching." We employ more accountants than any other nation. If we were to be hoisted on our own petard, that would be our penchant for numbering. Anton Chekhov made a trenchant observation about words, but it may apply even more to numbers:

> *"One can prove or refute anything at all with words. Soon people will perfect language technology to such an extent that they'll be proving with mathematical precision that twice two is seven."*

We assume that words are less precise than numbers. But you can prove or refute anything at all with words as well as with numbers. Maybe more. Any clever person can lie with statistics, just as marketing experts and politicians do. They use words or numbers for their own advantage, rarely, if ever, for yours. But children are taught how to do this. Not only do they see their parents and other adults manipulating each other for their personal advantage, but they get dubious reinforcement for doing the same thing. Whatever else they may be, their tears are frequently manipulative. So are their tantrums. We need words and numbers to get to the moon, or beyond. But very few people you know…use words or numbers for legitimate purposes. If you are gullible, people will take advantage of you. If you are not, you may not fit in with those in your social circles.

Fleas have lives. So do elephants. So do mice and birds and fish. But they have neither words nor numbers to talk about their worlds, to create and maintain some sort of virtual reality. To repeat, Freud said that with words and numbers we people are capable of making our own hells or heavens on earth. This is as relevant to an individual life as it is to our collective destiny. A person uses the concepts (words or formulae) available to her personally to interpret and navigate her world. Any group of people having frequent verbal intercourse will share the perspectives of the majority of the group. Birds fly, fish swim, as the old adage goes.

They are largely hard-wired at birth to see their worlds the way they do, and to perform in them as they do. They have no cultural imperatives, which come from explaining things. People do. We may be animalistic. But over millennia we have become as much creatures of our cultures as of our genes. Perhaps even more so today. For example: People invented the "law of large numbers" in playing with statistics. With it came the notion of the "average." No bird or fish thinks of itself as average. That's a wholly human idea. As useful as it may be to mathematicians (who are busy with proving that $2 + 2 = 7$, as Chekhov chides us above), it has caused much trouble in our various societies. A meritocracy and an egalitarian democracy may not mix. We can explain why some people are superior to others. But not everyone wants to be the inferior one according to, say, the bell curve. Some people are taller than others. The remedy, Goldsmith satirized, is to saw some off of them so we can all be "equal." Statistical mathematics (surely a human invention) wants to differentiate people and things, by measuring large numbers of people or things. A liberal ideology wants things like people to be equal. Those can be antithetical. Similarly, no standard dose of any medication is the right dose for everyone, as we are just beginning to learn, even though our ancient forebears knew what *our* ideologies kept us from intuiting. Our many technologies are frequently not compatible with slower-to-change ideologies. This creates yet another kind of class society. Is it compatible with the notions we harbor about radical democracy?

+++++

We *measure* things. The more things we measure, the more we measure things. If your spouse or partner doesn't measure up to the images you imbibe in the upscale glamour magazines, is this a sufficient legal ground for divorce? Our legal system in the West is a culturally-inspired method for measuring the rightness or the wrongness of some action. We are far from doing an adequate job with the measurement tools (the laws) we have for doing so.

The measures we concoct are not arbitrary. Yet they do not arise from the nature of things. We may measure distance in feet or miles. But some cultures measure distances in terms of how many cigarettes are smoked from here to there. Our automobile instruments tell us how fast we are going (mph). But if you are driving in Europe, you would be travelling at so many kilometers per hour. If you wanted to buy something at the butcher shop, you would pay so much per kilo. A nautical mile is not 5,280 feet. And so on. Measures are culturally specific. And then so are the instruments that get invented to measure things for us. How far away our destination is can be determined by how long it takes to get there. But time and distance are also measured by how we think about them (and the perspective our instruments provide that make it unnecessary for us to think). It might seem that the few thousand miles that birds or whales migrate is phenomenal. But we put more miles on our vehicles every year than that. So we "migrate" further than they do. We commute, sometimes 2-3 hours a work day. Why do we? They migrate, sometimes for many days. Why do they? They have to. We have to...but for significantly different reasons. Will the reasons give you a better perspective on why people do what they do?

Protagoras said that *"Man is the measure of all things."* In this, he was mightily prescient. How could he have known that, in our wayward culture, we have been drifting toward social circumstances in which every person is the measure of all things – that each is entitled to his or her own personal opinion, and that all opinions are equal? What is presaged here is that the measuring device is also constructed by those who share the observer's perspective on things. As the philosophical physicist Werner Heisenberg put it:

> *"Since the measuring device has been constructed by the observer...we have to remember that what we observe is not nature in itself but nature exposed to our method of questioning."*

Or, literally, the perspective we stand on to observe our worlds and ourselves in them. Heisenberg was addressing physicists who wanted to better understand what they were actually doing when they made their observations. But it applies to all of us humans. The devices we use to measure things are consistent with the perspectives we bring to bear on our observations. If you dislike someone, your observations are biased to accord with your perspective – *perspective* being the basic framework of all observations made by people. Our method of questioning derives from our cultural and sub-cultural perspectives on the world. The world physicists see is different from the world a poet or a woodsman sees. None of us sees things as they are. We see things from the perspective we bring to bear. *What we measure by our devices is what we assume exists because our perspectives lead us to believe it. And belief asks for confirmation, not negation.*

+++++

Explaining "why" something did or didn't happen, whether to oneself or collectively amongst those who share a culture, creates a sort of *logic* by which future events will be explained. The mind is always at least marginally formulaic: for things or events to be comprehensible to people requires an explanation that "makes sense." And an explanation that makes sense is an explanation based on some algorithm which is reasonably consistent with past explanations. Perspectives are thus teleological. They reproduce themselves through use. They become what it is possible and necessary for them to become, given what they have become through past use. They are self-fulfilling because we are far more susceptible to their confirmation than we are to their disconfirmation. What doesn't confirm them is irrelevant, and thus passes unnoticed or avoided.

We all have a vague understanding of what is "logical" and what is not. When something strikes us as being illogical, it's because it doesn't conform to the logic that we have collectively and personally come to apply to our own perspectives on the world – and us in that world. It is other people who are illogical, not us. That's because we assess them and their actions by the way our own minds work, not theirs. Elbert Hubbard at his ironic best defined logic thus: *"Logic: An instrument for bolstering a prejudice."* If it weren't so logical, it would seem fair to conclude that all logic is prejudicial. Where one person's logic is not the same as another's, and where one culture's logic is not another's, conflict and differences of opinion arise. They do not share the same perspectives on the issues differentiating them, and perspectives, like premises, function as the logics being applied. Lewis Carroll must have offered us the telling example in *Through the Looking Glass*...when he wrote:

> *"Contrariwise," continued Tweedledee, "if it was so it might be; and if it were so, it would be; but as it isn't, it ain't. That's logic."*

At least in the popular culture of our time, what's logical correlates to what is "true." What is true for a person or a people is what is assumed (or ought to be) to be true for everyone else. If you refute someone else's logic, you are obviously bolstering your own prejudices – your own perspectives, your own premises. And, as Tweedledee is given to say, "if it were so, it would be; but as it isn't, it ain't." Our perspectives are prejudicial. Other people either see things as we do, or they are wrong. There is pure logic. And there is everyday logic. We use our everyday logic to navigate our worlds, and to pass judgment on others who don't agree with us.

Our logic – how we mentally connect things with other things – is thus much like a theory, or a hypothesis that becomes a part of our reality, and of our identity. It is a part of who we are. Who we "are" is a function of how we think about things. Our logic is how we connect ourselves to others and to the rest of our worlds, and to ourselves. Anything that challenges our logic is a small or large threat to who we are. We don't abide that kind of threat. In some extreme cases, it must be eradicated from the earth. Native Americans had their own clan logics (or truths). Since those truths were not based on European logic, those Indians had to be put on a reservation, to live or die. They fought back, because this was a threat to who *they* were. Who wins such conflicts is not who was right, but of superior firepower. We would be speaking Japanese or German if either of those had won that war. Then we would be the ones who had to learn a different way of thinking, and thus of being.

You use your mental models (the logics of your mind) every day for strategic or tactical purposes. You plan using the logic of your mind. You have expectations about what might happen as a result of what you plan to do or not do. You live mostly in the virtual world of your mental models. Change your mental models and your life has to change. Change your life, your mental models will adapt. It's easier to change your life than to change your mental models (the logics of your mind).

By observing us, clever people – like criminals, salesmen, marketers and politicians – will be able to detect our mental models, and use them against us. Our mental models, like highways of the mind, are private, as are our agendas. Illusionists figure out what they are likely to be, and this is what makes their illusions (or "magic") possible. Pickpockets size up their prey. They can detect the easy marks by clues that become *their* logic, just as politicians and other marketers do. A clever insurance salesman calculates what he has to do or say to sell insurance to certain people. In the stories written by Arthur Conan Doyle, Sherlock Holmes uses "Sherlockean" logic to track down the best criminals around. He does this by using *their* logic rather than his or the commonplace logic of the day.

So how one comes to explain the world to oneself might be efficacious. But it can also be detected by others and thus used against one in the social games we play. When detectives look for a "motive," they are really looking for the logic used by the supposed criminal. We are often either predator or prey in those social games we play. Our perspectives on things can be useful to us. But they also make us vulnerable to the unscrupulous that surround us. Our routines become ruts. And the ruts of our minds are where our mental models take the form they do. Clever predators can explain us to themselves better than we can explain us to ourselves. In *Middletown* (1929), Helen Merrell Lynd wrote:

> *"It is characteristic of mankind to make as little adjustment as possible in customary ways in the face of new conditions; the process of social change is epitomized in the fact that the first Packard car body delivered to the manufacturer had a whipstock on the dashboard."*

Epitomized perhaps also by the fact that the word "whipstock" may no longer be in your computer's dictionary. It was a holder put on wagons and buggies as a holster for the butt of the whip used to make the horses go faster. The first competitors for car manufacturers were not other car manufacturers but were horse-drawn wagons, which could make it across New York City faster than could a car. The logic of the automobile was fine. But the horse-and-buggy owners made more money by *their* logic.

+++++

Such perspectives enable us to go out into the world, or to play at introspection. There are as many ways of looking at our worlds as there are worlds and selves to look at. A recipe for social maneuvering is a kind of logic. But the world we live in is rarely as logical as we expect it to be. If our logic seems to work, we become bored. If it doesn't, we become distraught. To avoid boredom, we choose a different path. To avoid the dangers inherent in a different path, we choose sameness. Each is a perspective, fraught with its own unique possibilities and dangers. As Yogi Berra once quipped, *"When I come to a crossroads, I take it."*

> *"Science is a first-rate piece of furniture for a man's upper chamber, if he has common sense on the ground floor."*

-- Oliver Wendell Holmes

Perspective 8

A Brief on Lexicon

A *lexicon* (a term that has been around for a long time) is essentially the "vocabulary" used most often by a person, an occupational group, a clique, etc. It marks who we are and what subculture we belong to. It is also the outward evidence of how one's mind works. We should all know by now that how a person "communicates" (both inward and outward) and that person's mind are two aspects of the same thing. Our minds are created and evolve in how we communicate with the rest of the world and ourselves, written, oral, or otherwise. Thus one's capabilities may hinge upon how efficacious one's lexicon is given one's cause and purpose in life? Astronauts (and others) have to have the "right stuff" to be chosen. What is the "right stuff" for having life choose you? And what part of that right stuff is in your personal lexicon?

For example, if your lexicon is past-oriented, you are more likely to allow your past to determine your present. If your lexicon is future-oriented, you are more likely to be *pulled* into your future according to your perspectives on your future, as you express (and live) those. The past is dead and gone. It may leave you with some residue, if you allow that to happen. But life is in your future, not your past. When people fall in love, it is not their pasts that drive them. It is their expectations about their future that drive them. The more people talk about (or listen about) sickness and dying, the more likely it is that they will associate with people who would help in making that a self-fulfilling prophecy. Knowing from experience that words have consequences, ancient peoples typically made certain words taboo. If hate or envy cannot be a part of your lexicon, it becomes very likely that you will not perform those kinds of feelings. If revenge is frequently the crux of folklore of your culture or subculture, you will be inclined to make it a part of who you are. If your lexicon is success oriented, you are more likely to move in that direction. Once your lexicon (your mind) adapts to being a victim, you will practice that orientation in your life. If you believe you are going to heaven and not to hell, you will have a different perspective on life than does the person who believes (by talking about it) she is going to hell. If you can imagine a future life that you work at making come true, you will live longer than a person who does not have that perspective on his or her life. If you are a poet, you will have a different perspective on life than does a homeless person. The difference is revealed in that person's lexicon. If you are insatiably curious about what makes you tick and the world go round, you will have a very different kind of lexicon than does the person who knows all of the answers, at any age, in any walk of life.

If all you know is what you have heard on the local or global news, you are merely imbibing the lexicon of the news industry. If you imbibe the chatter of the world in clichés, and if your lexicon is laden primarily with clichés, you will become a cliché. If you want the life everyone around you has, you can attain that only by emulating what they talk about and how they do so. Your lexicon both enables and constrains your perspectives on your world and your life. What you cannot discuss with others or think about privately will be no part of your life. Your lexicon functions much like the architecture of your mind and thus of your feelings in and about your life.

+++++

Words are the building blocks of your mind and thus of your conscious life. A poorly designed building will be dysfunctional in one way or another. A poorly designed (or evolved) mind will similarly be dysfunctional. Anything about which you cannot speak or understand is something that will not be a part of your life. Your regularly-used vocabulary forms the parameters of your mind, beyond which you cannot know or experience. A word, spoken or written, is a word. In your mind, a word is more than a word. It is a concept. How you conceptualize yourself and the world you live in makes possible – or *impossible* – the life you can have, and how you will experience it. If there is no word for "friend" in your lexicon, you will not experience friendship. If you have such a concept in your lexicon, you will see and act in the world according to how you conceptualize it. If you had no word (concept) for "enemy," you could not have enemies. If there were no word for "depression" in your collective, would it be possible for you to perform being depressed? Would others in your collective comprehend you if you did? How, indeed, would you perform being depressed in public if you had never seen it performed? Words are not just your windows on your world. They *are* your world. You do not perceive yourself or your world and then put names to it. You see and experience yourself and your world in and through the lexicon you have for doing so. As Montaigne averred so fundamentally:

> *"Our understanding is conducted solely by means of the word...It is the only tool by which we communicate our wishes and our thoughts...if we lack that, we can no longer hold together; we can no longer know each other."*

It is not exactly so. The verb "communicate" is tricky. People take you into account not only by your words but by who you *are* (ineffable as that may be), by your reputation, by your dress, by your possessions, by your status, by their history with you, etc. It is people's interpretations that account for any communication encounter, not what *you* say, or do. You cannot know with any precision what people mean by what they say or do. And you are constantly taking the world (and those other people) into account. You live by your interpretations of what is going on. So do they.

As prescient as he was, Montaigne omits here the most fundamental form of communication – and that is talking to oneself. You need a lexicon to do so, and you need a lexicon for making sense of what you say to yourself. This self-reflexivity is just as important (even more so) than how you perform yourself before others. Society would not be possible without the words that comprise a lexicon. But neither would humans as we know them be possible. It is difficult to imagine that there is anything more critical to our lives and our societies than how we explain our worlds and ourselves in them – how we create perspectives through lexicons that are efficacious and not deleterious. *A lexicon – personal or cultural – that is not hygienic is a lexicon that will lead to mental, social, physical, or spiritual dysfunctions.* That is, an unhygienic lexicon can lead to psychopathic disorders, and it can lead to sociopathic disorders. It can also be part of the etiology of physical disorders of many kinds, and of disorders of the spirit. Thomas Carlyle wrote: *"Be not a slave of words."* What this may intimate is that the person who is not the master of her words will be the slave of her words – her lexicon.

And Shakespeare may have offered what is most hygienic about words, lexicons, and communication when he wrote:

> *"There is nothing either good or bad, but thinking makes it so."*

We dictate our destiny by how we talk about things, how we explain things. These are in our thinking because the meaning of things is the mind's work. The meaning of things we impose on things will determine our trajectory in life. The words of our lexicons are not just words. They are the source of the meaning of life, and everything that happens. As a culture, we have not gone the way of Marcus Aurelius. But he put it well:

> *"Get rid of the judgment, you are rid of the 'I am hurt'; get rid of the 'I am hurt,' and you are rid of the hurt itself."*

Or, as Eleanor Roosevelt once quipped, something like this: "No one can make you feel bad without your permission." It gets to the point of not being a victim of words, or of your mind's interpretation of things that happen in your life, without your permission. Want what happens, Epictetus advised, and your life will go well. That's one basic way of making your lexicon more hygienic. But in any case, the interpretation is yours to make. You can either use the pop culture interpretation which you have seen many times, or you can provide the interpretation that is most hygienic for your life – the one created by you to be efficacious for you and everyone around you.

+++++

Mark Twain said, to put the right point on lexicon:

> *"The difference between the almost-right word and the right word is really a large matter – 'tis the difference between the lightning-bug and the lightning."*

In our permissive society, we have come to think that a word is a mere conveyance, and that one word is as good as any other word. Because we are too lazy or too indifferent to make the effort, if we don't quite understand what we're talking about, we insert the expression "ya know" multiple times in every blah-blah we fall into. By doing so, we lead ourselves to believe that it's the hearer's responsibility to make good sense of what we're saying, that inarticulateness is a relatively innocent way to make or to keep friends in our social circles. It may indeed be. If we speak in clichés, as we have previously considered, with people who speak to us without the capability of thinking through what *they* are saying, we can indeed bond – with others who are similarly mentally disadvantaged. Twain thought it was his duty to be articulate – to be able to use the right word in the right place. This required having many words at his command. He suggested (in the above) that calling a bug a lightning bug had nothing to do with lightning. If you confused them because of the one word "lightning," then your lexicon is not very hygienic.

The "right" word is like opening the door to a different perspective on oneself and one's world. The "right" word is like stepping into a right world. As Wittgenstein put it:

> *"Uttering a word is like striking a note on the keyboard of the imagination."*

We must keep in mind that any person's imagination in both enabled and constrained by her lexicon. The better and the richer it is in its efficacy, the more and the better one's imagination. But in using that metaphor, Wittgenstein had something even deeper in mind. If the word strikes one as harmonic – in keeping with the life desired – it will enable one to further the music of his/her best life. If it is discordant, it will lead that person into blind alleys and detours, neither of which can contribute in any intentional way to the life one desires to live.

Your lexicon is not only the source of your communication with your world – both for understanding and expressing yourself in casual or critical encounters. It is also the only source you have available for talking to yourself, for thinking through a serious problem, and for making you who you are. If you want to be someone other than who you are, you have to change your lexicon. It will be difficult to impossible to do that without changing your epistemic communities – the people you most hang out with, whose lexicons you will inadvertently or purposefully share. If the people you hang out with – in person or via some medium like books or artworks or films – are the people whose lexicons offer you a better life, then you are on the right path. If they are not, then you may be on the wrong path. Again, consider well (and imaginatively) these:

"The limits of my language mean the limits of my world."

--Ludwig Wittgenstein

"As the stamp of great minds is to suggest much in few words, so, contrariwise, little minds have the gift of talking a great deal and saying nothing."

--La Rochefoucauld

Perspective 9

Assessing the Efficacy of Cultural Perspectives

We are all born into some kind of social group – a clan, a tribe, a community, a nation, an immediate and extended family. We are first exposed to a language, a way of thinking about and doing things, a way of seeing the world from that perspective, and a way of fitting into (being socialized into) that perspective on the world. Two people will create a culture. More people will create a more complex culture – one that is more influential because everyone else more or less accedes to it. A culture constitutes an infant's first imperatives for comprehending and navigating its world – in consciousness, perception, and tastes. Mental and physical diets used to vary greatly from culture to culture. So their people were different. Globalization is a form of homogenization. Through contact, we are becoming more like each other, by creating a hybrid which is neither one nor the other, but something that evolves from the mixing of cultures. Different philosophies emanating from the past may have concerned themselves about where our cultural perspectives are leading us. The demise of such philosophical concerns in our hybrids – where other more immediate things seem of greater importance – leaves us bereft of such vital concerns. We do what we do. Our destinies as persons or societies have faded from our conscious concerns. We are more concerned with sex, self-indulgence, entertainment, and having what other people have than with where this leads us. Our long-term best self-interests get lost from view in the muddle of our busy days. People might wish that they were someone else. But hardly any do anything about their discontent. The more "freedom" we have, it seems, the more perverse we get.

+++++

Someone once said that trying to identify the influence of the culture and the subcultures one is embedded in would be a bit like trying to bite one's own teeth. To do so requires that a person has to use his or her own mind to try to assess those influences. And they are already an indispensable part of the mind that might attempt to assess itself. To question a belief requires doing so with a mind that is already formed around that belief. To have a perspective on the world (or oneself) means standing on that perspective in order to assess that perspective. Even if that were possible (which in our Western episteme is not), we would have to stand on some other unexamined or taken for granted perspective in order to examine the one we want to assess. We have to see the world (and ourselves in it) from *some* perspective. That becomes a given in the process we have to use to examine it. What our cultural and sub-cultural perspectives provide us is an explanation of things that have to be taken for granted in order to examine other things.

There are two conditions in this insoluble conundrum that cultural anthropologists have identified: **one** is that in order to understand fully or validly another culture, you have to belong to it, in which case you are no longer an observer but a member of the group you are studying. You are stuck with trying to assess yourself with the influences that (unseen and therefore not chosen) make you who you are.

The **second** is that you can only see the effects of the culture in which you are embedded from the perspective of another, different, culture. The observations made by those cultural anthropologists were made from their perspective, not the perspective of those they were studying. In other words, if you want an "objective" interpretation, ask the observer and not the observed. On the other hand, if you want a "subjective" interpretation, ask the observed and not the observer. This has been for years the bugbear of psychotherapy and psychiatry and, of course, the making of judgments about others in everyday life. Do we ask them who they are? Or do we ask people other than them whose opinions we value?

The social skills required to gossip in our culture are understood to do so without including the person being gossiped about. Our cultural perspective is that a person's reputation is determined by those who have an opinion, excluding the person himself or herself.

It's a strange perspective. But most cultural perspectives have a certain strangeness about them when they run counter to what little rationality we can muster. There is sexual coupling in every culture that is likely to perpetuate itself. But the protocols and customs for doing so can vary greatly from culture to culture. Like cannibalism, what is customary in one culture may be unacceptable in another. In our peculiar culture, we have elided love and sex, sometimes using the terms interchangeable. It was not always so. Before the invention of romantic love (c. 12th-13th centuries A.D.), sex was sex and romantic love was not thought of. After its invention as a part of our lexicon and thus of our thinking, it became one of the most problematic things about our lives. Given its consequences, was the elision a good thing or a bad thing? For example, in the 1989 film by Nora Ephron, *When Harry Met Sally,* there is a scene in a restaurant where a woman witnessing Sally acting out an orgasm to make a point with Harry said to the waitress, "I'll have what she's having."

To those of us embedded in our cultural perspectives, it calls for a laugh or at least a smile. To those in another culture, who may go about topless or in penis-enhanced garb, it may be a source of embarrassment. Then there is the issue of envy: how much is enough? Envy *was* one of the seven deadly sins. But there is plenty to go around in our culture today. Envy is tolerated. Sex in public is not. Zsa Zsa Gabor was reported to have quipped on one occasion:

"I know nothing about sex, because I was always married."

Again, this may be taken as humorous. But that may hide the point she was trying to make – that married women were not supposed to know anything about sex in her time. From different cultural perspectives, sex is an open and healthy thing. In our culture, it was not long ago something to be censored. We can represent it by innuendo, but calling things by their raw names is not acceptable. In some cultures, it is the most common swear word. In our own culture, until recently, women who smoked in public (once taboo) never spoke of it in public. Simone de Beauvoir, one of the West's earliest feminists (who don't exist in some places where they are not culturally encouraged to exist) wrote in *The Second Sex* (1950):

> *"Sex pleasure in woman...is a kind of magic spell; it demands complete abandon; if words or movements oppose the magic of caresses, the spell is broken."*

All of which is to suggest that cultural perspectives on something as basic as sex are relative. But then all cultural perspectives are relative, not to any reality, but to one another. In any culture, our cultural perspectives become our truths, our realities. They are socially-created and socially-maintained. We judge others (and ourselves) not by who or what they or we "are," but by what our cultural perspectives dictate. Because they are ubiquitous, cultural perspectives are also insidious. Since we are immersed in them 24/7, they become a part of who we are almost like osmosis. They seem "natural" to us as we grow into adulthood. Almost by the time they start to school, children have imbibed the larger culture and the particular epistemic communities to which they belong at their most plastic age. People who grew up in the South begin to sound like Southerners, and people who grew up in New England begin to sound like Northerners. Not only do they speak a different vernacular, but they have certain perspectives on the world that are different. Someone born and raised in New York would, if transported to the Deep South, would feel like she has been beamed off into an alien world. And *vice versa*. Perspectives not confirmed by those around you will make you feel that way. That's the insidiousness of cultural perspectives. Historically, civilizations come and go. This means that they are not self-correcting, nor are their perspectives efficacious. The Aztec perspective on the arrival of the Spanish conquistadores led to their demise. (Their perspective was that the Spanish on horses were the warriors who were to come to protect them, according to their prognostications.) We may think of ancient peoples as being ignorant. But they were no more ignorant than we are. We have our cultural perspectives, developed in our stories and our folklore. They are not necessarily efficacious. They will take us where they go, not where we should be going. What politicians (or friends) do you know today who run on the destiny of our civilization? It is a vital subject lost in the pell-mell busyness of our days. For example, feminism and radical equality still influence our social policies and our opinions. But Charlotte Perkins Gilman, in her 1898 *Women and Economics* reminds us that –

> *"There is no female mind. The brain is not an organ of sex. As well speak of a female liver."*

Her perspective on such things is not the cultural perspectives of our day. The question is: Are our social movements efficacious with respect to our destiny? Are they taking us where we should be going, or simply where they are taking us? Are we any happier or healthier for the social movements of the past century or so…or not? (To repeat: A perspective that functions to improve your life or the destiny of your society is *efficacious*. A perspective that does not do that is not efficacious. So that's how cultural perspectives need to be assessed.)

People who have a cause and purpose for their lives that they are pursuing have a very different perspective on the destiny of their society and their own lives than do those people who are not pursuing a chosen purpose in life. As the number of people who are not pursuing a purpose in their lives outnumbers those who do, the destiny of their societies, as well as their own, begins to head South. That's because cultural perspectives are created and maintained by the people who belong to that culture. It refracts them and their perspectives just as they refract the cultural perspectives that they use every day. This is as much the case for a marriage of two people, for example, as it is for a society of thousands or millions. When there are as many subcultures as there are people who create them and join them out of some disaffection, there is no longer one overarching cultural perspective. As William Butler Yeats famously wrote in *Michael Robartes and the Dancer* (1921):

> *"Turning and turning in the widening gyre*
> *The falcon cannot hear the falconer;*
> *Things fall apart; the center cannot hold;*
> *Mere anarchy is loosed upon the world…*
> *The best lack all conviction, while the worst*
> *Are full of passionate intensity."*

Those who once had conviction are so outnumbered by those who have none that things begin to fall apart. And the "center," which consists of the guiding cultural perspectives in traditional societies, cannot survive. They cease to exist in the din of what was once referred to as the Tower of Babel – a world occluded by fragmented knowledge and opinions, and just too much "infotainment" and indifference to the consequences. By the "worst," Yeats is not referring to bad people. He is alluding to all of the good people who have no purpose in life other than to be driven by the events of the day. They are merely floating downstream with all of the flotsam of the day to a destination they have no conviction about – either for themselves or for the societies they belong to. They are passionate about whatever the happenings or the social movements of the day can be used to arouse their idle passions.

There have been human cultures (now mostly gone) whose cultural perspective was that nature was sacred. Our (mainly Western) perspective is that nature is something to be subdued and controlled. These are radically different perspectives fomenting radically different ways of living. Given the sheer longevity of such cultures as the Australian Aborigene (c. 40,000 years) and the American Indian (c. 35,000 years), it may be obvious that our Western episteme is not as efficacious. The

Navajo, as a further example, did not believe that "progress" was the most important element of their culture, but that "beauty" was – as in their refrain about everything they did, "And let it be done in beauty" (repeated three times). We don't even say that about marriage, or work, or play. They lived differently because their cultural perspectives were different. They had reasonably effective medicines, based on trial-and-error. We have reasonably effective medicines based on "science," but far more powerful (like our guns). They are also based on trial-and-error in a laboratory, but may be lethal in actual use. They knew from their cultural perspectives which mushrooms and berries are poisonous. Most Americans outside a grocery wouldn't have a clue. Because we are a money economy, there are many hidden agendas at work in our systems. When the perspective is the health of the tribe, there were certain duties and responsibilities that do not exist in our Western perspective. Health and happiness to them was their duty to the tribe. Ours is something we are told we can get only if we pay for it.

In the purview of Western "science," sickness or disease is caused by conditions over which people have little, or no, control. The American Indians generally believed, with Seneca the Younger (5? B.C. – A.D. 65) of whom they probably knew nothing, that ...

> *"Having good health is very different from only being not sick."*

There are very few physicians (more recently licensed in the U.S.) who would understand this. They are actually taught the opposite. Western medicine is a high-status occupation. Hippocrates said that no physician should advantage himself (or herself) by the misfortunes of others. That's part of the Hippocratic Oath, taken but rarely adhered to by those who take it in order to be licensed. In a world in which there is no "economics" of sickness and health, people and their predators see that world quite differently. It isn't that one is right and therefore that another is wrong. The current trend toward what is called "Integrative Medicine" is based on the perspective that there are alien and ancient methods of perceiving health and illness that may be as efficacious as

Western medicine. Some people think that their doctors are gods. So some doctors perform that role.

In *Poor Richard's Almanack* (November 1739), Benjamin Franklin wrote:

> *"Nor is a Duty beneficial because it is commanded,*
> *but it is commanded because it is beneficial."*

Not necessarily, as we know more recently from those who did their duty in the Nazi gas chambers. The knights of the Age of Chivalry put their duty before all else, as did the Samurai of Japan. And when they didn't, as we know from the myth of King Arthur, the whole society (in this case Camelot) fell apart. Our own cultural perspective has to do with freedom and equality, not with duty. The average citizen of America has no responsibility for those five generations out. Some American Indian tribes had the perspective that they were responsible for the world in which their progeny, seven generations out, would be living. Again, it is not that one cultural perspective is right and therefore that any contradictory perspective is wrong. It is simply that they often make for very different ways of life.

So it is that cultural perspectives creep into us because we are immersed in them. To us, they are merely "reality." They become a part of who we are. If we have no responsibility for our own lives and our future, we will live our lives very differently than if we did have. There is something ominous about having no such duty to our tribe, or to ourselves. When freedom becomes freedom from responsibility, as is happening in America, the world thus wrought may be the kind of world none of us would want to live in. Other planets may appear to offer an alternative. But wherever we go, we take our cultural perspectives with us. If *they* cannot save us, no alien, cultureless planet can.

+++++

Once a central cultural perspective has rooted itself in us, we look for confirmation of it, not a challenge to it. That is part of culture's insidiousness – we find our beliefs and values refracted in our world. We find what we are looking for. And we see only what we are capable of seeing. We see our propensities refracted in those around us – keeping in mind that we chose them for that purpose. We see our propensities in the other artifacts of our lives. A street with no sidewalks may suggest that walking is not an option, requires a vehicle of some sort. City folk are used to traffic congestion. It is just a part of their lifestyle. We see tall buildings in big cities. They are possible only because elevators were invented to make them so. Recent research suggests that young people, who spend hours looking at photos and texts from "friends," have to be trained to deal with people face-to-face. There are young children who believe that milk comes from the grocery store. Are there any grocery stores on Mars? We "have to" go to school. We "get to" play. Which one is more appealing? These are all simple examples of our cultural perspectives. The world we inhabit is physically a given. So are most of our thought-ways. If a highway is built, people will take it. If a way of thinking gets widespread traction, we will take it.

+++++

Our cultural perspectives are essentially our reality. A video of animals in the wild is more real to most people than would be an animal in the wild, which most have never encountered. Our cultural artifacts include the movies and virtual realities of play stations. There is much violence portrayed there, chosen by their customers. They may say they think war is terrible, but they enjoy playing it, observing it safely on a couch or theater chair. We may say we believe in romantic love. But sometimes that turns into hate. Both are portrayed dramatically in films. We seem to be able to justify either state of mind, of being.

A people's culture used to grow out of the realities of their every day lives. This is no longer so. The popular culture is enabled by all of our technological devices for making artificial life more real than real life. We know that movies are manufactured like cars are manufactured. The parts are put together for dramatic effect – and for cost saving. Our own lives are not manufactured. They emerge from the way our minds work. And if our minds work like that of the director of a film or the amateur smart phone photographer, that is what we will be exposed to. That is what we are immersed in. We can consume manufactured stuff on our various devices for doing so. We can even imagine that people who are shot get up and walk away at the end of the scene. The popular culture has become our culture. It's no longer an archive of the wisdom of the ages. It is there to entertain us and to arouse our feelings from which we take our opinions. The pop culture is not a considered one. It is the sediment left behind from the thoughtless consumption of our entertainments and our "news." We want electronic gadgets that will think for us. Computers are believed to make us smarter, faster. They don't. The opposite may be true. But in any contest these days between what's good for us and the popular culture, bet on the pop culture.

So when we look upon the events of the world, we see them through the lenses of the popular culture we are accustomed to. We do not see what is there – as much as we pretend to believe that. We see what we expect to see, and that comes from the perspectives of the pop culture that we regularly imbibe. What we "see" in the world around us is not what's there. We see and understand our worlds according to what our perspectives make possible – and necessary. Our cultural perspectives lead us to believe that there can be "rights" in our society without responsibilities to that society. That's possible, because more and more people believe it. But it probably predicts to a dysfunctional society... which we may be getting glimpses of in the news of the day. It has been noted over several years that we spend more for "healthcare" than does any other nation on earth. In a society where one has a right to do anything one wants about their own health, but someone else is responsible for paying for the consequences, the "health" of our society could increasingly be in jeopardy. Cultural perspectives do not move in the direction of making any culture healthier. Cultural perspectives do indeed have consequences, but not always the ones we want or need.

+++++

Like many other commonly used terms, the term "culture" has more than one meaning. It originally connoted something like the repository of do's and don'ts for the people belonging to a tribe or nation – their traditions, their customs, their morality, the source of their individual consciences. With the rise of the "cultured" class came the conceit that culture referred to the finer things in life – fine art (as opposed to "folk" art), literature (as opposed to popular reading), opera and ballet, classical music, archery, and high-fashion dress and cuisine. This tells us more about social class than it does about perspective, except that the perspectives on such things by the leisured class was, and remains, different from the common person's perspective on the same things. Tastes constitute an interesting foray into what it means to be human. But what we want to focus on here are the rules that emerge in any human grouping. They were as important to the human hunter-gatherers as they are to a modern marriage or the social media. Those "rules" are ways of thinking about the world and oneself. They are inherited from others. Every marriage has a more or less unique culture, as does every clique or larger organization. They emerge from a kind of tacit consensus about how to feel about things and how to perform oneself in public. They are our shared perspective on everything we assume we need to have a perspective about.

If you are reading in order to pass a paper-and-pencil test, that's one perspective. If you are reading just to kill time, that's another perspective. If you are reading to be entertained, that's another perspective. If you are reading in order to enhance the *quality* of your life, that is yet another perspective. With which perspective you engage in order to "read" depends primarily upon the group or class or clique or occupational category you belong to. When he was talking about *"The culture of distraction"* in a Jean-Pierre Barou interview for the *New York Review of Books* in 1989, Andrei Sakharov was referring to *"mass culture,"* the one that provides more distractions than what anyone may *need* to know. We are bombarded by the sheer capacity of our electronic (digital) technologies. How rare in the many texts you might receive from your "friends" is one that brings you what you *need* to know? That's the culture of distraction. If you've "got mail," it must be attended to, not because it may be meaningful to your life, but because it might be meaningful to your continued employment or relationship.

+++++

How do your perspectives change? If you relocate to a different culture, your cultural perspectives will change. If you relocate to a different marital partner, your cultural perspectives in that particular culture may change. If you are told by your doctor you may die, but you don't, that will change your perspective on things. If you change your place of work, you may have to change your perspectives to "fit in" that culture. If you change the people you most hang out with, your perspectives will most certainly change. You were not born with any particular cultural episteme. That gets seeded by the people who brought you into this journey – your life. It will be nurtured to some state of fruition or decay by the people you talk to most, the people who are most important to you...past, present, and future. Recognizing that cultures are made by people, Sartre wrote in *Les Mots (The Words)*:

> *"Culture doesn't save anything or anyone, it doesn't justify. But it's a product of man: he projects himself into it, he recognizes himself in it...."*

First, people make their cultures. Then they make themselves in their images of them. If we like who we've become, we take credit for it. If we don't, we can always blame it on our parents or our society or the cultures we inhabit, which provide us with continuous enculturation.

With apologies to Sartre and his words, culture may not justify, but people often use it to justify their peculiar ways of thinking and feeling and doing. If the Devil is a part of your culture, you might be able to excuse your actions by avowing that "the Devil made me do it." Joan D'Arc claimed that God told her she had to do what she did. People didn't really believe her until she began winning her battles with the enemy. Then they could imagine that she was heaven-sent. Who or what should be to blame takes away from people the obligation to choose what they think or do. In a speech at Simon Fraser University in 1973, Arthur Erickson offered an exemplar of this displaced responsibility:

> *"North American civilization is one of the ugliest to have emerged in human history, and it has engulfed the world… This great, though disastrous civilization, can only change as we begin to stand off and see… the inveterate materialism which has become the model for cultures around the globe."*

It is not we who are to blame. It is "materialism." You can't live in a consumer-based economy, democratic or not, unless you pursue a perspective of materialism. Well, "you" could, of course. But then if the path you have chosen turns out to be wrong for you, wouldn't you still have rampant materialism to blame? Certainly you wouldn't blame yourself for taking the wrong path. This brings us around to Stanislaw Lec's pithy remark:

> *"No snowflake in an avalanche ever feels responsible."*

An avalanche, like a wayward culture, is a collective thing. It may be made up of individual snowflakes or concerns, but it is not controllable by any one person. No one you know was responsible for the culture that engulfs us. And neither you nor anyone you know can be (logically) responsible for halting or reversing it. Avalanches, like minds and like cats, have a mind of their own. They provide us with comfort and a degree of self-security. But changing them midstream is not something that can readily be done. The avalanche will cease when it is done tumbling downhill. The cat will find its perch for napping, ignoring you. You might be concerned about the "disastrous" direction our civilization is taking. But other than sermonizing, what can you do?

+++++

If you were to lose a basic cultural perspective, you would be losing part of who you are. If your spouse dies, you are no longer a part of a couple. You are now a single person, just ask the receptionist at any restaurant, or arranging a cruise. Let us assume you did not kill your spouse, so you are innocent. Does that change your perspective on the world and yourself? How others see you is sometimes more important than how you see yourself. You might try to perpetuate your previous identity through fantasy. But then your friends would assume you were hallucinating (which you were in the first place), and begin to question your mental health. You may grieve your loss. That may make you feel better...or worse. You may question your guilt in what transpired. But, believe it or not, nothing you do can change anything that has already happened. Our cultural perspectives may suggest that we should revere the loved one who died. But maybe we should have revered them more when they were alive. Some cultures do. We are missing what we once thought was ours. There are cultures whose perspective is that the spouse who died was not a possession. He or she was a guest in your world. We live our lives differently as a result of the cultural perspectives that have become a part of us. In some subcultures, the loss of one's car can be justified as more devastating than the loss of one's spouse. You can always get another one of those. A famous biologist once said, *"Things are the way they are because they got to be that way."* Nothing you do can change what has already happened. One may mourn the loss of what was once his or hers. The spouse who has died may have preferred not to be dead. None of that changes the actions of the avalanche, or what has already happened.

+++++

The flip side of the loss of a sustaining perspective is gaining one. Cultural anthropologists have long advised us that having no alternative makes the culture one has inhabited for her life appear to be the only "true" one. Becoming familiar with another culture is the best way of assessing one's own, from the distant perspective provided by that other culture. So perspectives are as well taken for granted until there are other perspectives from which the taken-for-granted perspectives can be seen.

So it is that gaining other perspectives – through reading or habitation – enriches one's *being*. And so it is that people who know only the cultural perspectives they live by are more militant about their "truths." Some people (like cultural anthropologists) know from their own experience that all cultures are relative. They are made by people and not by any reality. This is as much the case with every marriage as it is for every civilization. In *Patterns of Culture,* Ruth Benedict offered a pertinent observation:

> *"From the moment of his birth the customs into which [an individual] is born shape his experience and behavior. By the time he can talk, he is the little creature of his culture."*

It is in gaining the perspectives of another culture that enables a person to see his own culture for what it is. You have to assess your own perspectives from the perspective of a different culture. Everyone who remarries following a divorce has experienced this – for better or for worse. Every book written in English before you were born comes to you from at least a slightly different cultural perspective. If it was written long before you were born, it is likely to be from a significantly different cultural perspective. If it was written in another language, it will be even more challenging. The less familiar a reader is with the cultural context in which a book was written, the more of her own cultural biases she will apply to her interpretation. An example: In our popular culture, Machiavelli is largely misunderstood. That's because those who teach it (who would voluntarily read it when there is an American football game on?) are not familiar with the cultural context in which it was written.

We like to think that words are words and that what has happened in the world can be fully understood from the standpoint of our own cultural perspectives (imperatives). This is *not* the case. It is also the case that we cannot understand our own cultural biases except from the perspective of other cultural perspectives. In his remarkably prescient

Public Opinion, which was written about the time that "public opinion" was beginning to be recognized for the force it has become, Walter Lippmann wrote:

> *"In the great blooming, buzzing confusion of the outer world we pick out what our culture has already defined for us, and we tend to perceive that which we have picked out in the form stereotyped for us by our culture."*

We do not see what is there. We see what we have been programmed to see by our culture, in the form in which it has been stereotyped. The mind works with stereotypes, rarely with the raw world out there. We stereotype ourselves (with the help of our cultural perspectives), we stereotype others, we stereotype everything that is or that happens, in order to understand it. What we understand is our stereotypes of the world and us in it. What we don't understand is everything that doesn't fit our stereotypes. If a person operates outside of the stereotype we have of that person, we blame the person. If the world operates outside of our stereotypes for how it should operate, we blame the world. If we operate outside the stereotype we have of ourselves, we are diagnosed as having some sort of mental "illness." To be *well* in our culture, we have to play by our cultural perspectives.

Assessing our cultural perspectives requires what is referred to as "cleansing" in the East to knowing *why* one is who one is in the West. Unless it is your intention to be a better person than you are, knowing why you have been made the way you have been made is an exercise in introspective futility.

> *Perspective: A mostly unexamined way of looking at things.*

Perspective 10

Epistemic Communities

Until fairly recently, the culture into which one was born and socialized was the largest epistemic community. With the ongoing "globalization" of the many cultures that still exist, two great seismic consequences have been slowly, inexorably, and challengingly occurring:

- One by one the many human cultures that have preceded us have become – or are in the process of becoming – extinct. The many wars and "ethnic cleansings" that have occurred and are occurring are testimony to the death of many cultures to make way for the seemingly inevitable evolution of the coming global culture.

- The other impetus for such people's inhumanity to other people who are "them" comes from the struggle for hegemony – a struggle for whose customs and beliefs will become the dominant ones. It could be a conglomeration of those who make it through the struggle for dominance. But in those struggles that come with contact and commerce with other cultures, it is the victorious ones whose languages and customs survive. Values and beliefs have to come from some human source. And that human source is often the impetus for dominance. The victor in the culture wars may adopt some customs from the defeated culture.

The ongoing "Westernization" of scores of other cultures is an example of nonviolent (complicit) encroachment, which sometimes erupts into violent confrontation. The language and the customs of an extinguished culture that constituted a way of life has but remnants of its life-ways left in our version of human history.

More human cultures have become extinct than exist today. We like to believe that we have gained. But it is more likely that we have lost. We go to great lengths to try to preserve the animals and other critters on the endangered list. But we do not do the same thing with human cultures, which were a way of life for their people before being done away with – one way or another. Snow tigers have a way of life. We have to protect them and help them to flourish in our world. We don't see the role we play in the extinction of human cultures in the same way.

It seems that every epistemic community wants to be superior to every other epistemic community. If a clique or club won't have you as a member, you have to find another clique or club to belong to. Rich people don't relish socializing with poor people. Plumbers don't stand in line to join the social circles of those who have a higher status in their society. Vets returning from war find it difficult to fraternize with people who have not "served" their country – and vice versa. Professors prefer fraternizing with other professors, not students or staffers. Chefs prefer the company of other chefs, not often of their customers. Support groups are made up of people who have the same problems. Poets and artists prefer their work over the company of people who do not understand their work – just as CEOs do. Democrats prefer the company of other democrats, just as information technologists prefer the company of others who think like they do, and have the same problems.

What this is all about is that different people have different perspectives, and that different perspectives make them into different people. We gather in manageable-sized groups to confirm our perspectives – our different ways of thinking and doing and being. We have to get our ideas about how to think, how to believe, and how to feel from somewhere. And that somewhere is the social groups we have belonged to or that we presently belong to. In the modern world we don't learn much from raw nature. That's because we have less and less contact with nature. We have more and more contact with the people we work with, live with, text with, consume on television, or hang out with. We live in the virtual worlds we create in our intercourse with people. That's where our perspectives are seeded and evolve as we change partners and dance (communicatively) with others. The more such intercourse we have with others who have the kind of perspectives we do, the more certain we are that we are right. Being confronted with alien perspectives is uncomfortable. We avoid such confrontations when we can. We much prefer the comfort of being with like-minded people. Because our need to belong comes from our prerequisite need to have our ways of minding our familiar world corroborated by others, we sign on where we fit in. *Belonging* is thus a way of preserving *our* status quo – the status quo of those others, and therefore the status quo in general. We join or form epistemic communities in order to avoid such threatening challenges to who we are.

+++++

We have brushed up against this notion of *epistemic community* previously. This would be a good time to explore what it might really mean to us.

Epistemology, as we all know, is all about a theory of knowledge – particularly with regard to its methods, validity, and scope. So much for a philosophical perspective on what we know, how we come to know it, and what we can do with what we know. What we are far more interested in here is a pragmatics of where we get our "knowledge," how valid it might be for our purposes in our modern worlds, and what it has to do with our perspective on things.

An epistemic community is therefore a bunch of people who share a common knowledge, who defend its validity, and who also share their ways of gaining their collective knowledge and assessing its scope. In other words, all human knowledge is prejudicial, created by people for people, and is justified by the number and prestige of the people who ascribe to it. A tribe or a clan isolated from the Western world would be an example. They collectively "know" everything they need to know to get on with their lives. The size of the modern world may make any such singular episteme impossible. So over time cultures have splintered off into subcultures, and those into factions. The Western Church may be a good example. Early on, there was essentially but one church. Then there were two. Now there are dozens of factions, with splintering still ongoing. The people who share an occupation constitute a kind of epistemic community. They have their own unique myopia in common. Information technologists, like farmers and house builders, have their own relatively unique perspectives. They even share their own argot – their way of talking about things which sets them apart from other folk. Physicians use words that are derived from the Latin, thus further distinguishing them from their patients. Specialists in every field come to have their perspective on things, which gives them a place to stand to create their own facts, their own knowledge and their own ways of creating that knowledge and its validity…for them. Academicians are good at this, in much the same way that appliance repair people are. We have, indeed, fulfilled the myth of the Tower of Babel. Specialized lingo is the coin of the various epistemic communities these days.

Whose truths are we to believe? We believe the truths of the epistemic communities we happen to belong to. This is as true for marketers, who are busy establishing "brands" as it is for scientists, who are busy claiming to be closing in on the truth of things. They believe what their sub-factions offer as facts or truths. We are not arriving at the truth of things. We are arriving at the multiplication of the truths of things. In a permissive society, there are no limits to the number of epistemic communities that can be created and thus belonged-to.

What an epistemic community offers is a set of perspectives on the world, more or less exclusive to that network. It is a brotherhood/sisterhood for sharing beliefs and values, and offering a way of talking about those beliefs and values available only to those who belong. For those who participated in it, the Women's Liberation Movement was an epistemic community with a purpose. Some are more like guilds used to be. Christians do not share the same perspectives with Muslims. Those who belonged to the Mafia did not share their perspectives with the cops who pursued them, and vice versa. Pirates had very tight epistemic communities. They saw the world differently than did the naval forces that tried to hunt them down.

We (people) have to get our beliefs, our truths, our values, and our perspectives on the world from *somewhere.* They used to come from the one culture shared by your clan. Now they have to come from the particular epistemic communities you belong to, from one or more of the clans you belong to. In the film, *The Devil Wears Prada,* Andrea the ingénue belonged to her bunch of friends. Her boss weaned her from her clan and slowly introduced her to another clan, the one that would make it possible for her to be a significant journalist in New York City, which was why she came to New York in the first place. Her boss, Miranda, knew that who you hang out with fairly well circumscribes your potential in modern life. That was something which the younger Andrea had yet to learn. We all have to learn, sometimes the hard way, where our perspectives on the world come from, and what they make necessary but also what they might make possible.

That life lesson comes from understanding what part the epistemic communities we belong to by chance play in our lives. If we choose our memberships well, our lives will go well. If we choose our memberships poorly, or just fall into them through immediate need, our lives may not go as we would like for them to go. People who read the best books by the best authors belong to a vicarious epistemic community. Therein they learn how to read and how to express themselves influentially, surely a learned set of competencies that will do most people well in the lives they would really like to pursue. They can't get this from consuming the junk fare on junk radio or television, or by listening to their "friends" who may be operating from self-defeating perspectives.

We are ultimately social animals. It makes a difference in life which society you belong to. All epistemic communities are not equal. It makes a great difference which ones you belong to. Most have no interest at all in whether you succeed at the game of life. The feeling of belongingness is not enough. Epistemic communities will either advantage you, or disadvantage you. They may make you feel better. But no epistemic community is neutral, providing perspectives that have no consequences. Any socialization or education that does not enable you to distinguish the one from the other has failed you.

+++++

How could you "know" what the other people you regularly talk to don't know? It is the case that the "knowledge" created by those who create such knowledge continues to fill the archives established for storing it. It is also the case that every epistemic community produces an argot (slang) and clichés to sling at each other to determine who is in and who is out of the community. Sometimes those proprietary ways of talking become fashionable in the larger society. This doesn't mean that people in general are growing what they know that they need to know. It merely means that they are imitating what they have heard. It may change the way they talk in public, y' know. But it does not make them any more competent as human beings.

We have a cultural tendency to elide the meaning of knowledge with the meaning of intelligence. But they serve very different purposes. In *Abe Martin: Hoss Sense and Nonsense,* Kin Hubbard wrote:

> *"Intelligent people are allus on th' unpop'lar side of anything."*

Here, he is making a distinction between what constitutes popular knowledge on the one hand and intelligence on the other. Just because someone read somewhere that seven new "planets" have been discovered and passed this knowledge along to others, who passed it along to others, does not make anyone in that chain of information sharing intelligent. Nor did it add to the intelligence of the sky-watchers who made that discovery. They comprise, after all, no more than one more specialized epistemic community, for whom knowing that and sharing the instruments that make it possible for them to know that is not much different from a child sharing a secret with a friend. One question

Hubbard's observation raises is this: Will knowing that enable you to live a better life on earth? Or does such esoteric knowledge have only to do with one's status as a cosmologist?

You are bombarded daily with bits and pieces from the troves of our burgeoning "knowledge" about everything and anything It is actually data, since it is made to seem meaningful by someone in *some* epistemic community – such as the news business – for the purpose of making it enticing to you. Since it is unlikely to be of any other practical use to you, you will use it to talk to others about it. And thus the ongoing internal struggles in any modern society are likely to stem from which epistemic community is to emerge as the hegemonic one in the larger society. If we all know the same thing, we all belong to the only epistemic community there is. If we don't, we will belong to one splintered epistemic community or another. We all need a home base from which to try to recruit others to our opinions. Our own society is divisive because we take the position that all opinions are equal – *but only* if they are *our* opinions.

+++++

Epistemic communities are the source of our knowledge, as well as the source of the "approved" methods for generating and distributing that knowledge. The whole process of gaining and spreading that knowledge is thus legitimated. All knowledge is a way of explaining things. And, as we know, how we explain things in a given society determines the trajectory not only of our personal lives, but of the life and destiny of the society. No people's knowledge store has a way of cleansing itself. It may be displaced by more compelling knowledge. But it has no way of eliminating the knowledge that has been replaced – unless you are inclined to think of history as the dustbin of knowledge.

In our culture (in the West generally), we are inclined to assume that the newer a bit of knowledge is, the better it is. In this, we have obviously been influenced by our penchant for progress and obsolescence. We like to believe we are marching toward the ultimate truth of things. We are not. Knowledge is created by people, not by any nature we know of. Knowledge emanates from one or more epistemic communities. It is not inherently driven by any moral or visionary purpose for its existence, but by the proclivities of the epistemic communities from which it emanates. And there has never been an epistemic community that didn't have its own agenda. That agenda, or today that cacophony of agendas, is the course the life of our society will take, even if that leads to extinction.

At the personal level, there is an anonymous saying related to the exponential growth of knowledge in any society that has the perspective that more is better because it takes us to the truth of things:

> *"You can never know too little of what is not worth knowing at all."*

In the epistemic communities that guide the accumulation and distribution of what is called "knowledge," the main constraint is that of capacity. The more capacity they have technologically, the more they will collect and the more they will distribute. So we really don't get what we *need* to know, we get what they have to fill their offerings. It may be, for example, that there is really no "news." But you wouldn't know that by watching the evening news on television or by leafing through the newspaper.

The little aphorism above is actually very profound, and carries with it an important bit of practical advice. *You can never know too little of what is not worth knowing at all.* In the Western world, we get a surfeit every day of what is not worth knowing at all. That is in part because the supply far exceeds the demand. But what is probably an unintended result of consuming so much chaff that you can no longer really discern the chaff from the wheat. If your mind is filled with what is really not worth knowing at all, there is no room for what you might need to know. Add to that the fact that the mass media address their messages "to whom it may concern." They may not be addressed to you. We've already noted that people in general – even those who are familiars – can't tell you what you need to know. They can only tell you what they know. Cornered in an ongoing conversation, even most of your best friends will revert to what they happen to know. They have little or no interest in what *you* need to know.

But maybe that doesn't make all that much difference. Most people don't know (or don't care) what they *need* to know. So they are okay with the junk food of the day for the mind. When it is mainly for the purpose of giving them something current to talk about in case they fall into a casual conversation, it isn't its relevance to their lives that matters. It's the relationships they sustain by being able to talk about what others will be talking about.

In *A Study in Scarlet*, it was Sir Arthur Conan Doyle who wrote:

> *"Depend on it: there comes a time when for every addition of knowledge you forget something that you knew before. It is of the highest importance, therefore, not to have useless facts elbowing out the useful ones."*

If you are a fan of the logic that Doyle imbued his famous fictional detective with, then you know that Sherlock Holmes was a master at this. Holmes was famous for sorting out the useless facts from the useful ones. Most people can't do this. What is useful depends upon what you are trying to accomplish. If you have no particular purpose in mind for your life, then any fact is as good as any other – better if it has social utility. The capacity of our media is more or less infinite. The capacity of our minds is not. What's important can get carried away by imbibing in the tsunami of the unimportant to which most people subject themselves. It happens to us personally. It happens in almost every organization in which you might have a role – including marriage. And it happens to civilizations. In any society, when what's really important to its health and thus its survival gets lost in the torrent of words that come from endless, pointless opining, its survival is in jeopardy. Its health depends on the majority of its people pursuing worthy purposes. People begin to die when they cease to contribute to the welfare of the larger collective. And they take the civilization down with them. In his seminal study of *The Crowd* (essentially a modern phenomenon), Gustave Le Bon made this prescient observation:

> *"The acquisition of knowledge for which no use
> can be found is a sure method for driving a man
> to revolt."*

If that is so, then it would certainly serve as an explanation for why there are so many "demonstrations" for and against every initiative undertaken by people with a cause and people who are against their cause. It seems that people who have no cause of their own are the ones most likely to be recruited for a march or a demonstration about some current cause that is getting a lot of attention by the news media. They may not know much about the cause they are demonstrating for or against. But they know that the camera will be on and they might be on television, in much the same way as fans at a ball game will be most animated when the camera is pointed in their direction. It was the French writer Flaubert who once quipped:

> *"Some people commit a crime for no other reason
> than to see their name in print."*

In the past, we knew everyone who was on the same telephone trunk line as ours, or who shopped at the only grocery store in town. People went to the town square to be seen in the town square. We like our privacy, we say, but we need to be seen to be known as someone. We need to be talked about to be certain that we are who we think we are. As Katherine Hepburn put it –

> *"I don't care what is written about me so long as
> it isn't true."*

There is only one thing worse for one's sense of identity than being thought of as a nobody. That's bad enough. But what's worse is trying to be somebody that no one knows, or are totally unaware of. That form of isolation (or anomie) is often deadly. What Hepburn is implying is that being "somebody" in our world is somebody who is written about or widely recognized by image – a media celebrity. To be known by people who are "nobodies" is not very reassuring. So, in desperation, some people like that even murder other people or themselves just to be noticed by lots of other people in the newspaper, in gossip, or on the news. To be talked about makes you somebody. *Never* to be talked about is as dangerous to your self-esteem as shaking hands with a suicide bomber. Being noticed by others in a negative light is far better than never being noticed by others.

Who we "are" is a matter of how we have been in-formed by the people and groups we belong to. Those people and those groups of people are the epistemic communities we have belonged to and how we have been socialized within them in order to *belong* to them. We are largely and essentially products of the epistemic communities to which we have belonged, beginning with our parents and others in infancy. When we became sentient (that is, capable of interacting communicatively with our worlds), and as we began to use the language and the perspectives of those around us, they began to function like our parents once did. They become the virtual parents of who we become. What you choose to read, who you choose to talk to, what you choose to consume on television, and so on become the virtual parents of who and what you become. We like to assume we can choose who to become. But those epistemic communities mediate our worlds for us. Only within the limits that exist for us at any time in our lives can we forge our own existence. They do that for us. They are our parents. They make of us what they are made of. We become what is necessary within the perspectives of the epistemic communities we have belonged to...and what is therefore possible. To be somebody other than who you are, it is most likely that you have to change the epistemic communities you belong to.

+++++

We all usually assume that what we know is what we *need* to know. We have a tendency to assume that what we know is what is essentially knowable. When we converse with other people, we never give much thought to what *they* need to know. That's because we only know what we know. We don't really know what we *need* to know. We can't know what they *need* to know unless we ask them. And they…like us…may not know what they need to know. This is the conundrum about all advice, asked for or offered. Most advisers cannot tell us what we need to know. They, like all "experts," can usually only tell us what they know. Some financial advisers, unlike most doctors and pastors and friends and "the media," are better at this, because the better their advice turns out, the richer they become. Most of the advice we receive comes from people who are as incapable of dispensing worthy advice as we are of acquiring it. We shun wisdom in favor of being facile with the talk of the day. We prefer social status to life status. So we never learn how to discern the one from the other.

We don't seek advice from the indispensable epistemic communities we belong to. What we acquire there, without asking and almost by osmosis, becomes to us the truth about things – the perspectives about what's what and who's who that we cannot live without. An indispensable epistemic community to any person is one that he or she can't imagine being able to do without. We have pursued the issue of advice previously. What we want to recognize here is that the advice we internalize from our epistemic communities is not requested. It is just a concomitant of belonging, in much the same way that we do not solicit advice from ourselves. We just think and do what our epistemic perspectives call for.

And here is the conundrum: We all know what we know. As the social critters who are also the *source* of our knowledge – of what we know – that raises three fundamental questions:

1. What we know may just not be so – given that what we know is what we have explained to ourselves and each other.

2. What we know is usually such a tiny proportion of what we might create as our "knowledge," how can we know it is the tiny proportion we need to save ourselves and our civilization?

3. If the source of our knowing is actually not us, but what we actually imbibe from the epistemic communities we belong to, the only way we have to change our perspectives in any core way is to change the epistemic communities from which we get them.

In other words, the people or the media we hang out with parameters our knowing. We don't come by what we know by ourselves. Whether we "buy into" the right knowing is determined by the knowing we bring to the choices we make. Contrary thinking or knowing usually gets dismissed. It's possible we may be dismissing what it is we most need to know. What we know are our "truths." It's extremely difficult to see a better truth by assessing it from our own truths. We far prefer to assume that an alien truth is less reliable than the one that has got us this far. Sixteen centuries ago, St. Augustine asked, for any one who wanted to ponder his thinking:

"Why does truth engender hatred?"

Is it because there is, as far as different peoples (different epistemic communities) are concerned, more than one truth? Is the truth that the largest numbers of people believe the superior truth? We have already noted, with the help of the much-awarded geographer Jared Diamond, that civilizations may live by their truths, but sometimes become extinct by those same beliefs. Human truths offer no guarantees. As Daniel Boorstin argued in *The Image: A Guide to Pseudo-Events in America:*

"'Truth' has been replaced by 'believability' as the test of the statements which dominate our lives."

Boorstin was wise but rangy. What do you suppose he meant by that – back in 1961? So-called scientists still believe generally that they are in pursuit of the truth about this or that. Is the truth for this prestigious epistemic community mainly or only what to them is believable? Assuming they are people like the rest of us, how did they get to be exempt from Boorstin's pronouncement? Why is it that the Amish's truth is not the Congressional truth about health insurance? Why is it that a parent's truth trumps a child's truth? There is that diminishing clan on a remote island in the South Pacific who are far healthier than we are – but have no researchers in pursuit of the truth. Is it possible that there is a role for ignorance in healthy living (for example, they don't "exercise")? Or is Boorstin merely reporting on what is to him believable? In his *One Flew Over the Cuckoo's Nest*, Ken Kesey wrote:

"But it's the truth even if it didn't happen."

What are we to do with that, since we equate truth with our own experience of things? Since what we take to be the truth is always consensual (in our own epistemic communities), how could it be possible that truth could emanate from a disordered mind? When William James wrote about new truths, in his *Pragmatism,* that they are interpreted so as to show a maximum of continuity, he was talking about the likelihood that it is only our interpretations that are true or not. It seems undeniable, given how different human truths can be. So then the question is not: What is truth? But what "truths" do we need to insure our short-term and long-term health and welfare as a person or as a civilization?

In his inimitable way, H. L. Mencken averred:

"The average [person] does not get pleasure out of
an idea because he thinks it is true; he thinks it is
true because he gets pleasure out of it."

To facilitate our worthiest personal and collective purposes in life, is it possible we've got it the wrong way around in our own culture? Do we believe that fast-food for our bodies and our minds is the way it should be? Or is it merely the way "we" like it? Since there may be no such thing as an "average person," does that make Mencken's challenge false? Or, alternatively, true? As Mark Twain purportedly wrote in *Mark Twain's Notebook* (ed. Albert Paine):

> *"Truth is mighty and will prevail. There is nothing the matter with this, except that it ain't so."*

There are no truths that are not human truths. Even the Bible was written by humans, so far as we know. It is epistemic communities that create human truths. If there were but one epistemic community, there would be but one truth. But there is the Tower of Babel problematic: many epistemic communities create many truths. You will harbor the truths that are provided you by the epistemic communities you represent. Change those, and you change. Change them not, and their perspectives will frame your world.

It is not that epistemic communities are either good or bad. Without them, we would not be who we are. The vicissitudes of modern life will, like roadside attractions, take us this way or that. Life has whatever meaning we attribute to it. We have to get the meanings we attribute to life and our worlds from somewhere: either from the epistemic communities we belong to, or from ourselves. Neither offers a guarantee that the perspectives we gain thereby are the perspectives we need for a chosen rather than a happenstance life. If we only knew the consequences in advance, we might choose wisely. But since all of our knowing comes from the rear-view mirror, yet we have to live life forward (as Heidegger said), we may be stuck with living a life we didn't choose.

> *"Knowing the truth and living it are two things."*
>
> (Anonymous)

Perspective 11

Choices and Decisions

If life consists of one thing more than any other thing, it would be *choices*. If we tune into our lives, what we will observe there is that we are intermittently but constantly making choices. We choose the way we prepare ourselves to go out in public. We choose the clothes that hang on us or in our closets. We choose what we have for our meals. We choose the décor in our houses or apartments, just as we choose them. We choose our friends and our partners – not from the world at large, but from what's available. Even when we are making love, we may be thinking about (which we choose to do) what's next. Turning on a radio or a cell phone is a choice. What turns us on or turns us off are ultimately choices that we make. Whether we are good for ourselves or bad for ourselves comes from the kinds of choices we have made. We choose the place where we have been chosen to work. We choose the lotions and potions we buy. We choose how to spend the money we have earned from working at the jobs we have chosen. We choose what to do on this earth when we are not at work – since we assume that it is the people in charge who choose what we do there. But we usually choose what others have chosen – whether it is the books we read, the television programs we watch, the places we go to, or the clothes we wear. We also follow the fashions in how to pose for the camera. Pout-y may be in and grinning may be out – this season.

So are our choices *our* choices, or do we simply emulate what others that we look up to (e.g., our personal celebrities or people we presume to have higher status than we do) say and do? Do we simply recycle the choices that certain others make? We might even change our notion of what it's like to be "modern" by reflecting on a few lines from the playwright Euripides' *Hecuba* (4th-century B.C.):

> *"No man on earth is truly free.*
> *All are slaves of money or necessity.*
> *Public opinion or fear of persecution forces each*
> *one, against his conscience, to conform."*

So, for various reasons, we conform. Is conforming what we might really understand as a choice? Most people do not choose their consciences. So of what is each person a "slave"? Do most people choose the work they want, or the job they can get for money? And what is "public opinion"? Are we forced by public opinion? Or do we choose to be the slaves of public opinion – the opinions expressed by the epistemic communities we belong to? What are the perspectives we have that lead us to choose conformity? Closer to our time, James MacGregor Burns observed something very similar when he wrote (in *Leadership,* 1978):

> *"The price of group membership is conformity to*
> *prevailing norms."*

We have seen in the previous chapter how group membership is a human necessity. We have to belong to *some* group in order to think and feel and do as those in the groups we belong to have come to know and believe as they do – whether we belong by choice or happenstance. Being someone in some society requires us to ante. And that ante is our demonstrated willingness to conform to the norms of that group. Pirates had a code of conduct, just as do modern golf and church groups. You can't be a gang member without conforming reasonable well to the norms of that particular gang. The necessity to conform comes with the territory. You can't be who you *are* without endorsement by some group. The price that you pay to be somebody in your world is that of conformity to the prevailing norms of the social circles you belong to – or aspire to belong to. Hardly anyone in our modern culture goes topless or bottomless, which is the norm in some cultures. *We are known by the norms we perform.*

Unless you want to be labeled as a deviant of some sort, you will conform. Is that conformity a choice or just a tacit understanding? Would you choose to go against your conscience? Most people don't, because they no longer have a conscience to go against. If you want to think of yourself as "with" the prevailing norms of macro or micro groups, it is easier if you have no conscience to go against. Maybe that's the reason little effort is made to develop consciences in the socialization process. It might encroach on people's rights to be "free" – free of the constraints of conformity. Paradoxically, the freer people are of the constraints of conscience, the more necessary it is for them to be seen conforming to the prevailing norms of the social circles in which they move.

People in more traditional societies had norms, of course. But they didn't have to spend much time looking at others to determine whether or not they were in conformity. There was no alternative. Now that alternative lifestyles abound, you have to give more thought to whether or not you are in fashion (in conformity)...today. Thomas Fuller wrote: *"Do as most do, and few will speak ill of thee."* It may be that we live in a time where there is no "most" people. We are increasing fractionated by our opinions and the epistemic communities that people of all ages can belong to that an argument can be made for or against *any* perspective. People have always disagreed about incidental events. But these days a married couple can get into a down-and-out fight about whether something happened last Wednesday or Thursday, or about who said what and when – witness the film *The War of the Roses*. There used to be what was called a majority. No longer. We have balkanized ourselves into disputing anything and everything. What is "politically correct" may be wrong. And we're willing to go to the wire to make our voices heard – pro or con. We think people are interchangeable. They are not. We have come to believe that words are interchangeable. They are not.

Our carelessness about "free speech" has led us into a cacophony of heated arguments – rarely about anything personally important.

In his book about *Sigmund Freud's Mission,* Erich Fromm (whose perspective is useful if you want to understand the world you live in) wrote as follows:

> *"The individual in any given society represses the awareness of those feelings and fantasies which are incompatible with the thought patterns of his society. The force affecting this repression is the fear of becoming isolated and of becoming an outcast through having thoughts and feelings which nobody [will] share."*

If you want to belong, you have to pay the price. Perhaps "represses" is too Freudian. Over a long period of successful socialization into that society, the individual may no longer have the conscious fear of becoming an outcast. It has just become tacit: it is understood without thinking about it.

Socialization (particularly "proper" socialization) makes for perspectives that are just givens. It is improper or incomplete socialization that makes sociopaths. A psychopath never seems to know the difference between right and wrong (in that society). A sociopath knows the difference, but just doesn't care. To a sociopath, society is wrong. To a psychopath, doing harm to others is something they had coming.

Under the wayward burden of relativism, all human truths are considered relative – relatively equal, except one's own, which gives one the license to wreak mayhem on others, known or unknown. "They," those others, don't deserve the same license. We may like to think that all human truths are equal. But they are not – *in their consequences they are not*. Relativists of all stripes forget that. Conscience requires one to be responsible or at least feel culpable for the consequences. Free thinking does not. If you feel you are free to use whatever perspective you choose in your thinking and your actions, you are dangerous to the culture and subcultures you might share with others. And that means that you are first and foremost dangerous to yourself.

+++++

Some people use the terms choice and decision interchangeably. They may see choice as more immediate and capable of being handled on autopilot, or along the lines of how they feel at the moment. Decisions, they may believe, require more deliberation. In the modern world, where "teams" have taken over for individual incompetence, the deliberations of many may appear to be superior to the deliberations of one. That may be so. But it would depend upon who the many are, and who the one is. A person whose deliberations are wise is worth any number on a team whose deliberations are conventional. It's hard to get a smart decision from a dumb person. It's harder still to get a smart decision from a group of dumb people.

"Cooke's Law," in Paul Dickson's *The Official Rules,* may be good advice, but there seems to be no correlation between good advice and better actions:

> *"In any decision situation, the amount of relevant information available is inversely proportional to the importance of the decision."*

In other words, at the individual level, people are likely to acquire and ponder what toothpaste to buy than how they should live their lives. At the family level, a discussion of what color to paint the living room is likely to bring more information to the fore than a discussion about how to achieve a more efficacious family life. At the organization level, a meeting about what color toilet paper should be bought for the restrooms will usually garner a more passionate discussion than will the subject of how we are going to achieve our financial goals. People may talk endlessly about what they intend to do. But that is usually in lieu of doing anything about it. People may generally complain about the way their lives are turning out. But they will rarely make the changes needed.

+++++

For many people (too many), the process of decision-making gives them the feeling that the decision is the right one because of the way it was deliberated. They want to believe (and many do) that a "right" decision is more or less a guarantor of the outcome. No decision, arrived at in any way, obligates the future to turn out the way it is anticipated. It is a projection, nothing more. The amount of time spent deliberating a decision is often inversely related to the payoff. Some corporations still make 5-year plans. In our world, one year may be too lengthy. The best military strategists knew that when the first shot is fired, the strategic plan can be thrown in the wastebasket. That's because the interactions are dynamic. They are not subject to some pre-ordained rationality. We might assume that life is unfair if it doesn't meet our expectations. We overlook the fact that life isn't obligated to care one way or the other about our decisions. Nor are other people. You may decide to fall in love. But that doesn't guarantee any outcome. You may have fallen into the wrong rabbit hole. All decisions are flawed: not because they were not "properly" deliberated. They just have no special claim on the future. People who adapt to changing circumstances are likely to live longer than those who can't...or won't (those who believe their decisions deserve to trump the churning realities of life).

This may be what the Microsoft computer scientist Nathan Myhrvold was getting at as reported in Ken Auletta's article in the 12 May 1997 issue of *New Yorker,* entitled "The Microsoft Provocateur":

> *"Most decisions are seat-of-the-pants judgments.*
> *You can create a rationale for anything. In the*
> *end, most decisions are based on intuition and*
> *faith."*

Intuition? – meaning based on one's personal experiences in the past. Faith? – an interesting term to use in this context. It implies that decisions are based on faith in the future much like that harbored by religious fanatics. They are *certain* they are going to heaven if they do good, that they will go to hell if they don't – unless, of course, they pay for absolution in some way. Having an unshakeable faith in the future outcome makes one certain of her or his decisions in the present. But, being a computer "scientist," Myhrvold undoubtedly meant his observation to be taken in a purely secular way. He's suggesting that the myriad decisions we make in a day or a lifetime are driven mainly by intuition and faith. We make our decisions based on our "gut" feelings about things. All of the other data collection and deliberation we might engage in is merely window dressing. We fly through life by the seat-of-our-pants, which was the way the earliest pilots flew their planes: mostly intuitively and with faith in their judgments. It is the way we choose our mates. It is the way we choose our automobiles, our toothpaste, our apparel, and the way we express ourselves facially. For most of our decisions most of the time, they are not "rational." They correlate more with our feelings about things than with any pertinent facts. As Samuel Butler once mused about how our lives go:

> *"We are like billiard balls in a game played by unskillful players...."*

We hardly ever land in our intended pocket, except by a fluke. We may have good intentions, but our intuition and faith often do not serve us well. Without the skills to fulfill them, our good intentions are wasted wishes. Anyone can "wish on a star." But it takes far more than that to live a life of choice. Butler is making a generalization. We are not the one with the cue. We are the balls the unseen and unskillful players are trying to get into the pocket. The question is: Who (or what) is this unseen player? Best guess: they are the exigencies of life that occur outside of us. These are the tides and currents and seductions of the rest of world – which are indifferent to our hopes, fears, and intentions. To grow up is to arrive at the realization that the social and natural worlds outside of us just don't give a damn about our intentions. They have to be fought for in an indifferent world. We are buffeted here and there by forces we do not control, but which often control us.

The contemporary British writer Peter Robinson quipped:

> "...all life's important decisions are bets against the odds."

If the forces that we permit to mould and twist our lives were on our side, our intentions would not be against the odds. They are the unskilled players, influencing our lives, but caring not how our lives turn out. To win against the odds requires being skilled at life-making. We are not taught those skills. That's because they cannot be taught; they can only be learned. What would constitute the ability to make more efficacious decisions, given that *no one* is privy to their consequences in the future. Like Robert Frost, you could take the road less traveled. But if you do, the only thing you have to bet on is yourself.

One of Theodor Seuss Geisel (*Dr. Seuss's*) many aphoristic jingles was this one:

> "It's a troublesome world. All the people who are in it
> Are troubled with troubles almost every minute.
> You ought to be thankful a whole heaping lot,
> For the places and people you're lucky you're not."

No matter how troublesome life may be, there are always other people who have it worse. If there is a tornado some place other than where you are, you have justification for feeling lucky. You may feel that bad luck has singled you out. But you need only look around to find people who have more bad "luck" than you do. People may be depressed because they think they've got it bad. But what happens to us as individuals is essentially random. True, if you want to hurry things along, you can smoke or over-eat. You may do things that make you more vulnerable than you might be otherwise. But if bad things happen to good people, and good things happen to bad people, you can be assured that your feelings about things do not put you in control. It is your feelings that are controlling you. As often as this has been discovered, you might think we would all be aware of it by now. But our feelings get in the way of our understanding it.

+++++

It is the perspective we bring to bear on things that determines not only how we see them, but what we do about them – given our limited capabilities and our extensive incapacities. There is much, much more that we can't do than we can do. We may forget this when we are in the throes of making decisions or choices. Our popular culture would have us believe that if we could just make the right decision, all would be well from then on. There are two things wrong with that perspective on life:

- One is that the "right" decision is not determined by the procedure we use. Whether it was right or wrong can only be determined by how it turns out in the future. You can buy lots of advice that tells you what you should do, or how to do it. That advice may be useful or not, depending on how things turn out *in the future.*

- The other is that decisions don't fix things forever. Circumstances change. The decisions you make today will change the way things will be tomorrow. Decisions enacted create the need for other, often more complicated, decisions. As you change, so will your perspectives on the world change. We see the need for a decision through the prisms of our own perspectives. Maybe it's not a problem that needs fixing. Maybe it is an opportunity that needs grasping. It is our perspective that drives the need for our decisions. Maybe there is nothing out there that needs a decision.

As Ortega y Gasset once reflected:

> *"Living is a constant process of deciding what we are going to do."*

But maybe that is a perspective we have placed ourselves in by creating the complex and "modern" world we have explained our way into. Maybe it wouldn't have to be that way. The transitional character of Don Quixote thought so. He thought that life should be the way it should be. Truth-keeping societies (unlike our modern truth-seeking societies) never spent much time or effort on decisions about how to live. They already "knew" that. The only problem was behaving in such a way that their truths could persist. To be a truth-seeker is to be forever in a state of unrest. The truth, which will "set us free," is forever receding into the future as we are forever acceding to myriad ways of pursuing it. It is from the pursuit of something that the need for decisions emerges. Maybe the *truth* about the future is like a mirage. We see it in the distance, but when we arrive there, it doesn't exist. As Plato mused, *"No human thing is of serious importance."* Is it possible that our modern perspective – that all human things are of the utmost importance (as witnessed by "the news") – may lead us to assume that decisions on our part are far more serious than they actually are? Or that there may be things that are far more important?

+++++

In his provocative book, *The Paradox of Choice,* Barry Schwartz offers us several different perspectives on his theme: that the more choices we have, the more difficult and chance-y our choices become. And that the more money we have, the more paradoxical is the whole idea of a "right" choice. The subtitle of his book is *Why More Is Less.* It can be. Depends on your perspective, doesn't it? Some people have lots of financial resources, but still live their lives reasonably well. Others have little in the way of financial resources (for getting "more"), but still seem to live their lives reasonably well. If a person has been socialized to feel envious of those who have more than they do, or to feel superior to those who have less, they may fall into the paradoxical quandary Schwartz describes. But, in general (which is his perspective), the exponential increase in what we can choose as a way of life or a brand of tires creates perhaps not so much a paradox as a quandary that puts us in a position of having to choose and thus risk the likelihood of choosing wrongly.

Are we educated in such a way as to make better choices, no matter that there are more than ever before? The more choices there are, the more possibilities for choosing the wrong one. Would that explain why marriages lasted longer not so long ago? People didn't feel that they had an infinite number of choices. They had to choose from who was available. And in small communities, that was not many. The more choices we have with respect to the words we could use to express ourselves, it seems the poorer our choices. As Schwartz writes:

> *"...as the number of choices keeps growing, negative aspects of having a multitude of options begin to appear. As the number of choices grows further, the negatives escalate until we become overloaded. At this point, choice no longer liberates, but debilitates. It might even be said to tyrannize."*

Having more and more choices might seem to us a good thing. But it takes longer to shop at a supermarket than it did to shop at the corner grocery. Our choices about where to go traveling in our world are many times what they were in the horse-and-buggy days. Our technologies continue to increase our choices. But do we do a better job of choosing today than we did yesterday? It doesn't seem so. You can own 50 pairs of shoes. This leaves you with the problem of choosing which pair to wear today. That takes time and requires some mindshare. What could we be thinking about or doing if we weren't thinking about the range of our choices?

If someone goes to the grocery store to get something needed, and it is not on the shelf where it belongs, that person is now forced to choose an alternative product. This is what is meant by "We all live a life we didn't choose." Over time, our choices are thwarted for one reason or another. What we are left with constitutes the range of choices available. You may have wanted to marry the person who married someone else. You are left with what's left. And that's what you must choose from. After a while, the life you have to choose from is not the one you intended. It has been modified by exigencies over which you had no control. At any given time, the choices we make are within the parameters of what's available. We do not choose what we really want. We choose from the alternatives available to us – as we see them.

+++++

Perhaps the main conundrum of our lives is that our choices are cumulative, and our lives irreversible. We can't erase the choices we have made and start over. The choices we have made become the foundation for who we *are*. And who we are, in turn, becomes the foundation for the choices and decisions we *can* make, and therefore who we are likely to be in the future. People may be slightly or somewhat disappointed with their lives. But it is always much easier to continue on being who you are than to try to escape that in order to be someone else. We're familiar with who we "are." And most people will choose the familiar over the unfamiliar, oftentimes no matter how bad they think the familiar is. Battered women go where when they are released from the hospital? Back home.

The point is that choices are cumulative – meaning compounded. We might want to choose our way out of the life we have. But we can't, because in most cases of attempted change, people take who they are with them. Even in different circumstances, they are most likely to be who they were before trying to change. A divorced person may try his best to be a better person next time. But the pull of who we are is usually greater than the pull of who we imagine we would like to be. Who we are is the status quo. In any contest between change and the status quo, bet on the status quo. Achieving in life is always *in spite of*, never *because of*.

What you have to work with is who you are. And who you are is a cumulative amalgam of all of the choices you have made in the past. The philosopher E. M. Cioran had a way of challenging us with aphorisms like this:

> *"The most important decision you make in life is who to have as parents."*

We know that he knew this was not a literal possibility. What he meant by "parents" are those who directly influence the emergence and the evolution of our individual minds. They are the ones who make us what we are. We are choosing those people and those voices every moment of every day. If we choose well, our lives will be well. If we choose poorly, our lives will be the poorer for our choices. The problem is that choosing poorly anywhere along the trajectory of our lives leads to the accumulation of the consequences of those poor choices. But, then, if there are people who have not chosen Cioran as one of their parents, they wouldn't be aware of that, would they?

In *The Modern Theme* (1923), Ortega y Gasset wrote:

> *"The choice of a point of view is the initial act of a culture."*

What this can suggest to us is that a point of view precedes everything in life, from talking to oneself to talking to others to the media fare we consume. What we consume comes to us from a point of view. We interpret it from our point of view. What we "understand" is some amalgam of the two. This essential and prerequisite point of view is what we are here referring to as *perspective. Some* perspective gained through the choices we have made over time precedes all of our encounters with ourselves and/or our worlds. The meaning we attribute to anything and everything that is meaningful to us follows from the perspective with which we encounter it.

Another valuable perspective on our subjects in this chapter – choices and decisions – comes from the Czech playwright turned President of the Czech Republic, Vaclav Havel, in a 1988 Interview:

> *"God – I don't know why – wanted me to be a Czech. It was not my choice. But I accept it, and I try to do something for my country because I live here."*

It is sage advice for all of us. We live here. So we should try to do something that makes our country better than when we were dropped into it. It may not be one's choice to be here. But if one is here, he or she should try to do something for their country simply because they live here. There is this remarkable imperative that overrides our personal choices. They may be taking precedence because we live in that kind of popular culture – where the point of view may be that each of us is the center of the universe. For our own health and welfare, that perspective may not be serving us well. Havel admits he is not a Czech by his own choice. But he lives there. This alone requires him to try to do something for his country. That is a perspective that would make this world a far better place than it is. The world (or the community) we live in may not be our choice. But if we don't choose it, we lose.

As Carl Jung wrote in *Modern Man in Search of a Soul:*

> *"The great decisions of human life have as a rule far more to do with the instincts and other mysterious ... factors than with conscious will and well-meaning reasonableness."*

Those "mysterious factors" are the accumulated choices that we have made over our lifetimes. They become a part of who we are. They are the blueprint on the basis of which we get built. They are the perspectives that get called up to frame whatever it is we want to understand. They precede and inform our perceptions and the meanings we impose upon our worlds. The choices we have made become the fodder for all of our maneuvering in the worlds inside and outside of ourselves.

We don't just "choose." We choose from what our personal perspectives reveal to us as potential alternatives. We often don't "see" any alternative we believe we cannot fulfill. The consequences, as we interpret them, are also cumulative. From them, we derive the personal "theories" we impose on our worlds.

+++++

Our choices and decisions can also be seen as our personal attempts at deluding ourselves by interpreting them as a way of controlling the future. They enable us to deceive ourselves into believing the worlds we live in are more in our control than they actually are. They can be mental tricks that we play on ourselves. For example, you can "choose" to win the golf match. But that doesn't always happen. We can still plan to win the next golf match. We can "decide" to change our exercise routines or our eating habits. But given that our habits are better determiners of what actually transpires than are our intentions (our decisions), the results are not what we intended. If a decision was made but the consequences were not what we wanted them to be, has that decision really been made? Or is a decision not really "made" until the results are in? In other words, decisions need to be measured by the results, not by the process of making them. You do not control the future by making a decision. But you might create an aspect of the future if, and only if, your decision results in the consequences intended. If you decide that your mission must turn out as intended, it's time to do what needs to be done to "make it so" – as Captain Picard said.

You do not control the future, nor does the future control you. Word magic is notoriously overrated. You can't make a decision work as planned simply by talking about it. You have to do what has to be done.

Making your decisions turn out the way you intended requires doing triage as a prior but indispensable prerequisite. It is critical to know what the most important decision to be undertaken at this juncture, and which is the least important. Exigency is not a good criterion. What's happening at the moment may be less important than what has to happen tomorrow, or in forging your life for years ahead. What you can't control, you don't control. Triage may help. But life does not come with any guarantees. You might be able to *perform* your way into the consequences you want, if you have what it takes to do what has to be done. But you cannot *talk* them into occurring. When all's said and done, a person's rhetoric affects her more than it does any future. One's lexicon does not change the world. It only changes the perspective you may need to carry out your choices and decisions.

+++++

In our complex worlds, we are confronted with two perspectives on choice and decision:

1. One is your personal perspective on your choices and decisions.

2. The other is that the more than 7 billion people on this planet make choices and decisions every moment of every day, just like you do. The sandbox in which they play their mental and social games is the "real world." You don't control them. Sometimes they don't even control themselves – again, much like you. You may know less than a tiny handful of them. You don't control those few.

That's the good news. If you could control them as you control yourself, the world would be in greater turmoil than it is. The bad news is that most people (perhaps including you) don't know how to make efficacious choices and decisions. The world is like it is because it got to be that way. You are like you are because you got to be that way. You *could* change that by how efficaciously you go about making and implementing worthy choices and decisions. We have traded what might have been a very simple way of life-making for the onerous complexities of the mishmash that occurs when everyone wants to control the future with their choices and decisions. Epictetus wrote:

> *"First, say to yourself what you would be; then do what you have to do."*

If what we would be is *worthy*, and if we all had the capabilities required to bring that about, this would be a far better world for all of us. If your choices and decisions move us in that direction, you will have played well your role in life.

Perspective 12

Life's "Problems"

For a person to realize that he or she has a problem in life requires both a perspective on life and a perspective on what constitutes a "problem." As we all know, what one person thinks is a problem could to another person not be a problem at all. Yet happenings that potentially jeopardize our lifestyle do occur. We usually want a quick fix so we can move on without inhibitions or distractions. The problem we think we have is either physical or emotional...or in many instances, social. It is other people, things going on in the world, or random events that can affect some people as personal problems.

Perhaps the first thing to consider is that people have a need for *drama* in their lives. For some people, sometimes, there is too much drama in their lives. For others, the feeling may be that there is too little. If they feel like there is too little drama in their lives, people are wont to create it. If things become so routine as to be boring, people might actually *create* some drama in their lives. For example, marital bickering and arguments are assumed to be inescapable aspects of life's story (as told by the popular culture). When things become too routine, a marital or friendship spat may provide just the drama needed to get the adrenaline flowing.

The social part of it is that people who have more drama in their lives often get from it a boost in their social status. There is more social utility (as in banter at social gatherings) in sickness or fashionable social problems than in robust good health or in having only trivial problems to talk about. Other people have much more interest in your problems than they do in your achievements. If you don't have problems to talk about, you may be out of the conversation, where people are likely to be talking competitively about their problems. In other words, having the most serious problems puts you at the center of the conversation. Having no problems may make you into a wallflower. Being able to gossip about the problems of mutual acquaintances could save you. You can wax dramatic about others' problems.

So there is a need to describe your problems to others. Some people can develop this into a lifestyle – or at least into a performing art. They have a ready audience for this, because even hearing about someone else's problems has a way of feeding our appetite for drama in our lives. Some people can assuage their appetite by reading books about others' problems. Or, barring that solo experience, they can watch the most-watched television programs, which are more often than not based on the problems of the characters. This provides grist for the conversation mill. This was the premise of the very popular *Friends* series, and of most of the popular shows on television. That's why the Irish regularly visited their pubs: to share their problems, or the problems of the people they knew. Sports draw huge audiences on television. It is the drama based on who is going to "win" that draws us. Our "jobs" are largely without drama by comparison. At work, one rarely wins or loses big. It's all too rational. Office politics can sometimes raise your adrenalin, but only when someone else will listen to us bragging about our problems at work. Even the number of emails you receive can make you a temporary winner in conversation about such "problems."

Some people just have more problems than others. This puts them in the social limelight. The rest of us are willing to compete, and often do so by inventing dramatic problems to talk about. A near-death experience has a far greater dramatic impact than does the experience of a person who is actually dying. If you die, you are listed on the obit page. If you have a near-death experience, you might be able to dramatize it to the forefront.

All this is merely to point out that what raises your status is the dramatic impact of your problems. The people you know are likely hungry for the "details" – for the most dramatic stories about the problems other people are experiencing. That's usually what people are after in their favorite movies. Young people growing into adolescence can perform anguish about the most trivial matters. They are not dying of their problems – they are only sharing with intrigued others that they could have died of embarrassment.

If you have had serious problems – like cancer survival or being kidnapped, there might be a book or a movie in it, ghost-written by a writer who knows how to hold an audience in suspense. We all have our problems. They might have widespread and even commercial appeal if we can perform them very dramatically. Person A may shoot person B. That's fairly mundane these days. But if it can be told dramatically, then person A may become a temporary media and gossip celebrity (as in the tabloids). Where our need for drama in our lives meets our socio-cultural means of supplying it is where we experience our lives. The dramatic is exciting. Real life? Not often.

+++++

But let's say that you have problems that you are trying to *solve* rather than using them to gain social status. Then your perspective on your problems will be quite different. Even though you have an appetite for problems that satisfy your need for vicarious drama in your life, you may have problems you didn't want and want to be rid of them. Most of these will, of course be "people problems." Almost always, the person who will cause you the most trouble in your life ... is *you*. Then come those who are closest to you. But people you have never known can indirectly cause you trouble – like two strangers who are involved in a car crash at an intersection, or a robber who has been shadowing you for a few hours. If the fruit or vegetable pickers go on strike, the consequences can raise the price you have to pay at the grocery store. If you throw a stone into a placid pond, the ripples will spread outward until they meet an opposing force. If you engage in a marital spat, the consequences might affect your attitude for days or weeks to come. But they may also affect the lives of the people around you, like your children or the people you work with. But let's take a closer look at how and why such problems and their consequences get started.

Consider thoughtfully: If there were no people, there could not be people problems.

Maybe there would not be "problems" at all. Does the tree which is losing its roots and then falls to the ground dead have a problem? We (people) may say so, but does the tree say so? A fruit fly's life is roughly one day. Does the fruit fly see that as a problem? If the bird that smashes head first into your glass window dies on contact...no problem. If it lives on to fly another day...no problem. Most people do seem to have an irresistible need to have problems (drama) in their lives – whether socially or psychologically or physiologically inspired. They are sometimes rationally justified by their doctor or therapist. But sometimes they are not. By factoring in the need the explainer has for making a good or better living, the whole system begins to look like a game of cagey predator and willing prey. How the demand for expert predators creates the supply of willing prey is at least historically intriguing. Or is it the other way around: that the supply of willing prey creates the demand for the cagey predators? In cultures that do not have pharmaceutical industries, there appears to be less need for them. The point is that the two appear to balance out over time. Why should that be?

In his "A Servant to Servants," Robert Frost offered for our pondering:

> *"Len says one steady pull more ought to do it.*
> *He says the best way out is always through."*

There have always been other people like Len willing to prescribe a solution to the problems we tell them we have. What's changed is not that those solutions were free (they were not; reciprocation was expected), but that in modern times we pay some expert to fix our problems. If our gizzard is troubling us, we or our insurance companies pay the doctor to diagnose and prescribe a solution. If we are over our heads in debt, we pay some financial expert to fix our problem. If our car doesn't function, we pay some repair palace to fix it. If our love life is unraveling, we pay some therapist to tell us what to do about it. What once was a personal or a social problem is in our modern world one we take to some expert. We live in the age of expertise. Our problems are now commodities that are bought and sold in the marketplace, whether social or financial.

They may have been folkloristic. But the problems we once had were the problems that were being had by people like us. And the solutions offered were the solutions that other people said worked for them. Not bad. You may have encountered this before, but the satirist H. L. Mencken wrote, in *Prejudices: Second Series*:

> *"There is always an easy solution to every human problem – neat, plausible, and wrong."*

To guide our own perspective on problems, there are at least two implications here of value. **One** is that people rarely confront a problem for which they have (or don't imagine they could get) a solution. In fact, it is seemingly the case that we often identify a problem via its solution. The peddlers of their products for our exponentially-increasing ailments and discomforts use this as a formula in their commercials. They come bearing a solution to a particular product that they sell by describing its symptoms. We pick up two things from their commercials: these are the symptoms of a problem presently being had by people like you. And the product or recipe for eliminating your problem with ease is the one that you can buy from us. The number to call is .... Or, "Ask your doctor is our product right for you." The pull from solution to problem is compellingly done. What we learn is how to perform the symptoms of the problem.

The **second** is what Mencken means by "wrong." The solution was not wrong at the time. It is wrong now. It is wrong now because it is no longer is fashion. Fashions change. Fashions in the problems we believe we have and the solutions that encourage us to have them change.

Whether it's a manufacturing problem, a political problem, or a personal one, solutions change like fashions. And given our cultural perspective, we are likely to assume that a current problem and its current solution are superior simply because they are current. What's past is out of date. Families that stood in the way of the progress of love are almost extinct. When the child receives her first smart phone at about age ten and her first car about age 16 or so, she is no longer a child of her biological parents. She is a child of who she takes to be her peers. "Free love" has more to do with the availability of free birth control than was the case in the past. We moderns have our own ways of explaining things. One is that we don't have to be like our parents were. We reject one social trap by falling into another.

Because we solve our problems as we do, what results is more problems – and more complex problems. Solving a problem creates more problems and less malleable problems in the future. The evolution of society and our thinking about it has never gone in the direction of simplifying things. Progress is measured by the expansion (the complexity) of things, not their simplification. Permissiveness and complexity go hand in hand.

History is the march from simplicity to complexity at every level. This is especially the case at the level of technology. Shelley's *Frankenstein* is a cautionary tale. Robots are seductive workers because they don't cause people problems. But they do. Gloria Steinem wrote, in *Moving Beyond Words,* that:

> *"Clinging to the past is the problem. Embracing change is the answer."*

Embracing change may be the solution to somebody's problem. But it doesn't occur without creating new problems for them and for other people. It won't occur to you to try to change things unless you see the present – particularly one's own present – as a problem. Embracing change for a better future may be the answer to someone or some group's life. But apparently it does not change the need to use past words to express it.

Change is obviously not the answer to everything. There are things in the past and the present that perhaps don't need changing. For example, a person who really doesn't like her work is not going to like her work just because she changes the route she uses to get there. What would it take to get Steinem to change her perspective on things, as evidenced above. Gandhi had the perspective that if you wanted to change the world, you should change yourself. Is that really what she did? Is it change in itself that makes the world perfect?

+++++

No ideology offers a change that is necessarily for the better. We need a more pragmatic perspective on what constitutes a problem for a person or for a society, and how we (people) go about "solving" it.

- Do we find our problems in the symptoms of those problems, or in their source? We pretend that we are dealing with the source of a problem. But we are probably dealing mainly with the symptoms of those problems. There is little money to be made in obviating the source of our problems, when treating the symptoms can go on forever. To obviate a problem means eradicating its source in such a way that it won't occur again. Why do corporations have meetings to discuss the "problem" they discussed last week or last year? Why do people who have personal problems place the cause outside themselves and beyond their control? Why are personal problems so difficult to get rid of?

- We "have" a problem if we say so. This is most likely to be a problem that is being "had" by others – whether in personal or professional life. We describe it or enact it in terms of its symptoms.

- To deal with a problem requires that we give it a name that enables us to explain it. How we name a problem fairly well determines what we can or are going to do about it. The problem we name is not necessarily the real problem that needs solving. It is merely the problem we are now going to solve.

- The problem we identify is most likely to be a problem for which we believe we have a solution because we know a bit about such problems from past experience – or from others' experience.

- Thus, and most practically, the solutions we can bring to bear often determine the problems we have. In our own mindsets, we are all too often solutions in search of a problem.

- So far as we know, there is no inoculation for stupidity or for incompetence. To treat a psychosocial problem as a medical problem would be a little bit like treating a broken leg as a psychological problem. Every culture and subculture has its favored problems and its favored solutions. If there are lots of hospitals, people who are sick will go there. If there were no hospitals or pharmacies, would there be as much sickness?

- Different diagnoses might be helpful – as when a meeting is held in an organization to discuss "our" problem. Or they may not. The original *Physician's Desk Reference* had about eight pages of diseases, their diagnosis, and recommended treatments. Now digitalized, but in print it runs to more than four thousand pages.

- And that increase is just in the last three-quarter of a century. Imagine the size of that in a few decades into the future. Your doctor either consults herself or that resource to help her diagnose your disease. It is your symptoms that are being diagnosed, and thus treated, not always your illness (which might be a jeopardized lifestyle or just sheer disappointment in how your life is going).

- But consensus is just consensus about what to call the problem. Treating the problem comes from what we call it, not what it *is*.

- And the treatment of the symptoms will be more or less culture-specific. And...more or less whatever is in fashion in general, and whatever is popular in that particular epistemic community, as Steinem revealed. CEOs, for example, are more likely to be dealing with the symptoms that their peers and celebrities are dealing with, not any real organizational problem at its source. *Luck* always plays a role in business, as in life. Yet luck is rarely given credit for the way things turn out. We like to attribute our problems to causes beyond our control. But we still prefer to take credit for what *we* did if things turn out well.

- Problems seem to be the perennial palliative of choice for those who have too little worthy purpose in their lives, and too much time on their hands.

In his *Culture and Value*, Wittgenstein offered this (albeit metaphorical) perspective on our problems:

> *"If this stone won't budge at present and is wedged in, move some of the stones round it first."*

The problem he was addressing was this: Most people prefer a problem they can't solve to a solution they don't like (or never imagined). Given that for most people most of the time, it is a solution they bring from their experience or imagine they could get one from some source that informs their articulation of "the" problem. To speak of "the" problem leads people down the wrong path. There is no problem if it is not *somebody's* problem. If people think they have a problem, they do. Let them own it. If it is owned by an expert or a third-party payer, it will be interpreted by them. We are on the wrong path if we pursue a problem in the abstract – as if it were an objective fact. Problems arise from the perspectives we bring to bear on our worlds. The problem is not in the real world. It is in the perspective a person brings to bear on it.

By moving the stones around the wedged-in stone, he is pointing out the context in which the problem occurs – a problem being some discrepancy between the way things are expected to be and the way they seem to be. If you don't alter the context in some significant way, the unmovable stone will continue to be unmovable. The problem is not in the stone. It is in the context in which that particular stone is stuck. Fix that and the stone is free. For example, people are usually stuck in their ways of thinking about things. Change those ways. That's where the solution lies. If people in an organization, for example, persist in conventional ways of doing things – only trying harder – they are stuck in what the Chinese refer to as a form of insanity. The solution that reveals the actual problem lies in how the problem is changed by what is done about it – not in analyzing it.

If you are reading to learn, for example, the problem is abandoning yourself to where the ideas you are reading about take you – not critiquing the ideas by what you already know, or editorializing on them if you happen to agree with them. Learning is like the stone. You have to remove the other stones around it in order to free it from being wedged in by what you already know. As the "cynic laureate" of Finland, Erno Paasilinna, quipped:

> "The self-taught are the only ones who have learned. The rest have been taught."

If all you know is what you have been taught, to pass a pencil-and-paper test, you have not learned. If all you know is the commodity called the knowledge you need to regurgitate in order to move up a grade, you have not really learned. Since it is *your* interpretation you get from your reading, it is your interpretation that must be provoked into growth. It is not what to do that is life's problem. It is who or what or how to *be*. Schopenhauer put it in his pithy way:

> "A precondition for reading good books is not reading bad ones; for life is short."

To which we might add:

- A precondition for dealing effectively with difficult problems is not continuously dealing with the same old easy ones.
- A precondition for having the right friends is not having the wrong ones.
- A precondition for learning what you need to know is not imbibing what you do not need to know.
- A precondition for gaining the right perspectives on life is not gaining the wrong ones.
- A precondition for performing life well is not practicing how to perform life poorly.
- A precondition for seeing the world advantageously is not being satisfied with seeing the world disadvantageously.
- A precondition for learning is not depending upon others to teach you.
- A precondition for good health is not thinking, being, or doing what is unhealthy.
- A precondition for living a good life is not making relationships with those who do not have a good life.

And so on. You get the point. All of life's conditions have preconditions. If they are not the preconditions you need, you can't have the conditions you want.

+++++

So in solving our problems, what's to be done about the problems created by our solutions? *If you solve your problems in a conventional way, you will have the conventional results.* So we end up having the problems that others have, and trying to solve them as others have solved them. That's why our problems don't go away. We have something in common to talk about – our mutual problems. If you believe you have a problem no one has ever heard of before, not only will you not be able to get expert help, but no one you know will want to converse with you about it. The problems we have in and with life are typically the problems that are being talked about or written about. For the most part, there are no unique problems in life. There are only variations on the fashionable themes – variations on the problems in life that are being had and being popularly talked about.

As set forth above, if you have the conventional problems of the day, you will also set about resolving them in some conventional way. And the results will be the conventional results. In general, we don't extricate ourselves from our problems. We merely put a clever or a stupid spin on them. Then they appear to us to be new problems. We deal with them as we have dealt with them in the past. They come back to us in some modified form. And the spiral continues. Small wonder that our problems graphed over time look much like the DNA spiral.

When you "have" a problem, it becomes a part of who you are. And no matter that people may become quite disenchanted with their lives and wish they were someone else (as Woody Allen once quipped), we cling to who we are. As we considered before, most people prefer a problem they can't solve to a solution they don't like. The solution they don't like is the one that would require them to be someone other than who they are – that is, someone who doesn't have or hasn't had that problem. People and their problems are perversely related. As the columnist Evan Esar once observed:

> "We used to settle our problems over cigarettes and
> coffee – now they are our problems."

There is as much continuity in the problems a person or a society has as there is in the life of that person or of that society. Our problems evolve from our problems. The problems we individually or collectively concern ourselves with today have evolved from the problems we had yesterday and how we resolved them. Our problems evolve somewhat like bacteria. We make certain attempts to eliminate them, but they keep coming back in modified form. If the problem of global warming were defined as a problem in over-population and under-socialized life styles (given the consequences), we would be going about resolving it in far different ways. But it's much, much easier in both our individual and our collective lives to identify "the" problem as an objective one, outside of ourselves and our personal and our cultural predilections and perspectives.

+++++

So what are life's problems? They all depend upon what our epistemic foci are and what our predilections may be – from our beliefs to our tastes. In other words, what life's problems are depends upon who you are talking to, or listening to, or otherwise paying attention to. We've seen that big pharmaceutical firms can lead you, by clever and sophisticated commercials, to imagine you have the symptoms of a new disease for which they have the latest curative. We've seen that you may be required to fall in love and get married in order to "live happily ever after." There are no wildly popular stories about how you can live "happier ever after" if you *don't* follow that cultural prescription. We've seen that our perspectives on life come from the explanations that have been handed down from our forebears or from the people we hang out with or from our own feeble attempts. We've seen that the "real world" which we inhabit has not the slightest concern for our intentions or our troubles. We've seen that the human/social worlds we inhabit are made up but still have real consequences. We've seen that being incompetent or indifferent has its rewards in our world, and that it is only by trying to achieve that you can fail. We've seen that we are what we are, and that our worlds are what they are, because we say so. We've seen that we live in a vortex of happenings that we had nothing to do with, and cannot control. We've seen that we can't control randomness, but that we still have to face its consequences. We've seen that we have been disappointed by the leaders we have put in place, and the celebrities and experts that have put us in place, but we go on doing the same thing while hoping for better outcomes. We've seen that advice about how to live is ubiquitous, but that the advice-givers rarely follow their own advice. We've seen that life's problems are in the beholder, but where else could they be? We've seen that our perspectives on ourselves and our worlds lead us this way or that, but that a perspective on life carries no guarantee. We've seen that we would *like* to be good, but that in practice it often looms as being too much trouble. We've seen that a life worth living is easy to talk about, but for various reasons impossible to achieve. We've seen that bad things happen to good people and that good things happen to bad people, so that we sometimes feel like it just isn't worth trying. We've seen that when something bad happens to us it seems unjustified, but when it happens to people we don't like it does seem justified. We've seen that without a purpose life seems to be a crap shoot, but we've never met a person who has experienced our life as we have.

We've seen that pursuing a purpose in life brings extraordinary problems to the fore, and that having no purpose in life brings only ordinary problems to bear. We've seen that our perspectives take us where *they* go, with no regard for where we want to go. We've seen that (as Evan Esar says):

> "[people are] "...*forever striving to solve the problems of the world whose greatest problem they are.*"

So what are "life's problems"? We have been abjured from all corners of the world for several centuries now that...

> *We don't see the world as **it** is; we see the world as **we** are.*

Any other explanation or perspective seems (at least) empirically indefensible. The people who preceded us named their problems. Then they devised solutions for the problems they had named. The consequences of what they did make us, for we live in those consequences – they are the core part of the worlds we inhabit. A life is like that. We inherit the fruits of how our predecessors named their problems and solved them. They serve as the basis for how we see our own problems and what we might do about them. Because our times and the way we mind the world around us are unique, we add to the problem jumble what we see as our personal and environmental problems. And we attempt to resolve them with the only resources we have to do so: who we *are*. Who we are is the way we have come to see them, think about them, and do about them. Our minds are the limits of our worlds (to paraphrase Wittgenstein). American Indians attempted to solve their problems in view of the consequences five to seven generations out. We attempt to solve our problems (as we speak them into existence) for the present generation. That's a very great difference in perspective.

We have become more rational, more "scientific," in our perspectives on things. But, as George Bernard Shaw averred:

> *"Science is always wrong: it never solves a problem*
> *without creating ten more."*

It has perhaps always been that way. Except that in pre-Enlightenment times, only a new problem or two were created by how problems were named and dealt with. Religions attempted to simplify our worlds. Science inadvertently complexifies our worlds in exponential ways. "Artificial Intelligence" may solve a problem. But it creates dozens of problems in other areas of our lives. Birth control popularized may have solved a problem. But it created other kinds of problems for living our lives. That is the world that the television series *Seinfeld* (and to a certain extent *Friends)* explored. Our problems are often so complex that we don't even understand our problems, let alone their solution. All we seem to be able to do is differ about our opinions. It's as if we don't have the same destination in mind, even though we all ultimately have the same destination.

+++++

By giving our attention to certain things rather than certain other things, we choose our future, our destiny. If we don't choose the problems to which we give our attention, certain problems we may not want will choose us. Living one's life well requires choosing the problems you want to have, not having the problems that seem to be going around. If you live your life as a victim, you will have the problems that victimization has. If you live your life on purpose, your problems will not be the pop psych ones.

Sometimes what happens to us gets in the way of our purposes in life. When they do, it becomes a matter of choice. What remains your choice...*always*...is how you interpret what happens to you, or around you. To say you have "a" problem is not saying much beyond the fact that you have abdicated control of your life in favor of some prevailing perspective on it. To say you have a problem which it is your prerogative to name gives you optimum control over how your life turns out. Problems and life are two aspects of the same thing – they are not two different things. When you choose your interpretation of the problems that happen to come your way, you are choosing life. That's because how you interpret them determines who you will be. Some people give up as adolescents. Other people never give up. It isn't their problems that are different. It is the way they perceive them, name them, talk to themselves about them...interpret them. To have a purpose in life you are passionate and persistent about is the first step. Then, as the old musician said, *"Keep on keepin' on."* If you don't, you lose your "chops" – you lose sight of what you imagined your life was *for*.

If you have a life, you will have problems. What you permit them to mean to you is your choice. If you let them mean what most other people believe they mean, you have turned over your life to nothing more than the popular perspective on things. This makes you a victim of others' perspectives. To manage your own life, you must choose your own perspectives on things. That may be problematic. But it beats victimization. To be the pop culture's puppet diminishes your life. It is choosing your perspectives for your own worthy purposes in life that makes your life your own.

No problem can bring you down without your permission (to paraphrase Eleanor Roosevelt).

Perspective 13

A Life Worth Living

Who are we? Why are we here? How should we live? Why do we die? How do I come to know who I am? What difference does any of it make? What is one supposed to do with what we call our lives? Why do other people see the same world we inhabit differently than I do? Do we exist when no one else is thinking of us? What is it that sometimes makes a good life bad, and sometimes makes a bad life good? Why do we *feel* the way we do without intending to? Why does my life have the twists and turns and detours it has? Why me, rather than someone else? What is life, anyway?

Those are the kinds of questions asked since humans started talking to each other on this planet. They are still being asked. There is a good reason why. The first intellectual discipline was that of philosophy. Originally, all philosophies (such as that offered in the *Dhammapada* and other ancient texts) were devoted almost exclusively to questions of how to live. In the West, the Greeks made a street-corner business of it. It was the first "academic" subject to garner mass appeal. "How to live" may be touched upon obliquely in some academic disciplines today. But it has been relegated from its once key position to relative obscurity. Most modern philosophies shun such mundane questions. We are expected to learn how to live from the people we have lived with, or are living with, so there is as much advice as there are people who have fallen into a conversation about it. Or who pick it up from the popular culture, particularly the entertainment industry. We learn more about ourselves and our lives from stand-up comics and the movies than we ever learned in school.

It is presumed that our myths and our stories about such questions provide all that we need. Parents tell their children fables about how to live. Friends tell their friends stories about how to live. Gossip is about how we should be living. And most conversations (especially by cell phone) carry subplots and themes about how to live. We are inundated with direct and tacit advice about how to live. But many, if not most, people are at one time or another plagued with those kinds of questions. In *Conversations with Maya Angelou*, she is quoted as saying:

> *"I love to see a young girl go out and grab the world by the lapels. Life's a bitch. You've got to go out and kick ass."*

There's sage advice. But it's rarely taken. Most young girls would rather be "liked" than out kicking ass. Girls (and boys) would rather be liked than out grabbing the world by the lapels. In the film *Love Affair*, Katherine Hepburn is given this line:

> *"The trick in life is not getting what you want but in wanting what you get after you get it."*

Again, a potentially useful recipe. Reminiscent of Oscar Wilde, who wrote, in *Lady Windermere's Fan*:

> *"In this world there are only two tragedies. One is not getting what one wants, and the other is getting it. The last is much the worst; the last is a real tragedy."*

Is he saying that life is engendered in the wanting, but that the getting what one wants diminishes life in some way? And what of the modern world, where what we want is simply…more? And what about the person who gets what she wants, but ends up being discontent? Does it come down to wanting only what we need to live a good life – does wanting more than that become tragic in some way? What's the lesson here? Or do we simply no longer believe in tragedy? Do we live in our wants and desires, or in fulfilling them? And if you get what you want, what happens to your lust for life? Why is it that combat helicopter pilots report having more highs in their lives than do those behind the lines at their desks?

As if in response to Wilde, H. L. Mencken made this observation about life's "tragedies" in *Prejudices: Sixth Series:*

> *"The basic fact about human existence is not that
> it is a tragedy, but that it is a bore. It is not so
> much a war as an endless standing in line."*

In other words, the bane of human existence is not some banal personal tragedy, but boredom and the specter of boredom. In modern life, we might attribute much of our busyness, our diversions and our other entertainments to avoiding the pains of boredom. People have been known to fall in love (whatever the consequences) in order to avoid boredom. Rabid fanship and demonstrating with others about something or other are currently popular ways of avoiding boredom. It seems that most people are challenged by life. The few achievers there are challenge life. It has long been observed that it is those who challenge life who *have* more life. Does that recipe capture many followers? Apparently not. It has to do with how engaged we are with what we're doing. It seems that occurs most often from necessity outside ourselves. If we don't control the degree to which we are engaged in our endeavors, what is it that we do control? If people are not content with their lives, who should the complaint be directed to?

There is another perspective of concern that has often been observed over many years, and from many cultures: it is that many (if not most) people put off *doing* life in favor of talking about it – to themselves or others. We have plans, we have fantasies and intentions, hopes and dreams, but we never seem to get around to executing them. We may immerse ourselves vicariously in the lives of extraordinary people (or just our own favorite media celebrities). We may consume recipe after recipe from the self-help shelves. We may seek advice from our therapists and/or our pastors. We may even talk seriously about our lives with our friends over a drink or two. But, as the Spanish proverb has it: *"To speak of bulls is not the same thing as being in the bullring."* Some extraordinary people get in the bullring with the bulls. The rest of us come to watch them do so. We are more content to be spectators of life than to live it. This perspective is nicely captured by William Butler Yeats (in his "Closing Words," *Reveries over Childhood and Youth*):

> *"All life weighed in the scales of my own life seems to me a preparation for something that never happens."*

We are better at thinking about what might happen to us than we are at thinking about what we could make happen. So we never quite get around to living what we spent time preparing for. And what we imagined was going to happen never happens, at least never in the way we imagined it. We can't make happen exactly what we wanted to happen. But that may be because we were so engaged in preparing ourselves for what might happen to us that we had little time to equip ourselves for what we wanted to happen. People often seem to get more engaged in the preparations for their adventures than they do in the adventures themselves. Things rarely turn out to be as exciting as they seemed in our imaginations. Life is full of destinations which we rarely arrive at. And when we do, they seem to be a disappointment. There's a good reason why brides refer to their wedding day as the most important day of their lives. It rarely turns out to be as "perfect" as they had prepared for. Could that ever happen? Expectations that people have but don't have the competence to fulfill them are "dragons" that they carry with them wherever they go. To intricate others in your expectations is a way of reducing your responsibility for fulfilling *your* expectations by making them complicit in your expectations. This is sometimes the

MO in organizational meetings. Lovers often attempt to blackmail their partners by holding them "accountable" for *their* expectations. It is a subtle but potent bugbear in all human relationships. Many people don't even recognize that they are doing this, pleading innocence. Your expectations are your problem. To pretend otherwise leads to trouble.

+++++

Who are we? Why are we here? Most cultures have either a verbal or written explanation. These are called "Creation Stories." Those stories, dramatic or dull, are supposed to answer those questions for succeeding generations. They explain who's who and what's what. They explain how we got here, why, and what to do about it. Since they explain how we (people) got created, and how the world we inhabit got created long before any of us were born, we have to take them on faith. It is the kind of faith that holds a social group like a clan or a tribe together. People understand one another on the basis of the faith they have in that understanding. We don't get many of our recipes for living any more from our tribal stories. Those are outmoded. We believe in what's new. We believe in what other people we believe in...believe. The life that is worth living is the life that we happen to believe in. Science may inadvertently confirm our beliefs. If it does, then we believe in science. If it doesn't, then we move on to some alternative source of corroboration. Our perspectives on living vary with the ideas we fall in love with. We appear to be "modern" in that way. What we don't know is probably not worth knowing. In much the same way, a life worth living based in beliefs we don't have is probably not worth knowing about.

We didn't just get created once and for all. We are being created and re-created every moment of our lives. The more curious we are about how to live and the more we pursue that curiosity, the further it takes us in some direction. The ultimate security for us lies in our disdain for ways of life that are not those we believe in. If we believe in modern (popular, faddish) ways, the more we will ape them. The human dilemma has always been that of choosing a way of life that is not chosen for us. In a traditional society, there are no alternatives for which you will not be punished in some way. In a modern society, it is often living some alternative rather than the normative one for which you get to be more widely known. You are newsworthy if you are different in some public way. To fit in rather than stand out makes you forgettable. Status has to do with being different in some way – whether that is genetic or produced by air-brushing. If you don't grab attention by how you look or how you talk, you may be overlooked as no one in particular from nowhere.

There is no more than residual concern for who we "people" are and why we are here. Our concern seems to have been transformed into who "I" am. Over many years, our forebears invented gods so that they wouldn't be held accountable for the consequences of how we do or don't live. We moderns have dismissed them, or replaced them with technologies. We wanted to be free of any measure that was not our own. In *The Image; A Guide to Pseudo-Events in America,* Daniel Boorstin wrote:

> *"A celebrity is a person who is known for his well-knownness."*

The more people who recognize you by sight or sound, the more of their mindshare you enjoy, and you thus have the feeling of being somebody – of having an existence that matters. The less you have, the less sense of being somebody in this world of ours you have. Given how well-knownness is manufactured these days, who you "are" depends upon how you market yourself. We live in a culture based on marketing. Your influence depends not on where your influence takes your followers, but on how much of their mindfulness you can capture. The more risqué your dress, the more likely you are to be photographed. The more outspoken you are, the more likely you are to be recorded. The more people you kill, the longer you will be newsworthy. Celebrity doesn't have to be on the big stage. Every social group, every clique, has it celebrities – people being looked up to by people he or she looks down upon. In the *New York Times,* 25 April 1996, Maureen Dowd wrote:

"Celebrity is the religion of our time."

You may be challenged to keep up with the Kardashians. But not to worry; their command of their publicity mill will keep them well ahead of you. Our celebrities often get more obeisance than did our gods in earlier times.

In his *Heroes, Villains, and Fools: The Changing American Culture,* *Orrin Klapp* looked at it from a different perspective:

> *"The celebrity cult celebrates the triumph*
> *of ordinariness – charm without character,*
> *showmanship without ability, bodies without*
> *minds, information without wisdom."*

We live in a modern culture where "it doesn't matter what you are, it only matters what people think you are," which Lance Morrow took to be the fundamental rule of the Age of Celebrity. It's impression management that has become the measure of who you are. *What* you are is irrelevant.

There was a time in the past when people were measured by what they contributed to the larger society. Not in today's modern world. We are measured by how we perform our lives before those we want to impress.

The "those" referred to there, along with their celebrities, were perhaps better characterized by T. S. Eliot when he referred to us as "hollow." It's all superficial, not what any of the Creation Stories would have intimated. Klapp says that we ordinary people are bodies without minds, showmanship without ability. This may be in part our addiction to television: it's all performance, but better carried out than by our neighbors. And it's mostly all entertainment. "Life is too important to be taken seriously," as the old saying has it.

A now much-antiquated notion was that living the good life required character – a combination of competence and a well-wrought moral conscience. In the modern world, we take educational credentials and experience to be a reasonable substitute. They are not. Educational credentials do not guarantee good sense or even sensibility. And the value of experience is greatly overrated. Experience in lieu of an increased capacity for learning is usually either a deceit or a symptom of stunted growth as a human being. People today may carry about more information about things that are inconsequential. But the wisdom required for living well has disappeared. Farmers are more likely to survive a holocaust than are politicians or professors. In her recent book, artist Lauren Greenfield is quoted in an interview as saying:

> *"In our culture, a lot of what drives us is this quest for more – money, fame, beauty. This is an addictive quest. And you know it's bad, but you're still addicted."*

Her art as a photographer and filmmaker is intended to document graphically the growth of this addiction over time. There is no known evidence that conspicuous consumption ever leads to a good life. The poorest among us have often given us the best example of contributing to society – in poetry, in music, and in the ideas by which we live. Socrates may have gone about his cause in life barefoot. And his wife berated him for his silliness. But he and his acolytes are remembered, and she is not. The difference between living life and observing it at arm's length was once represented by Theodore Roosevelt as the difference between being on the playing field and being in the bleachers as a critic. It takes a long time to learn how to grow up. Increasingly, most people don't.

Voltaire quipped:

> *"To succeed in the world it is not enough to be stupid, you must also be well-mannered."*

Stupid people are obsequious. A good person is known for her deeds, not her servility or her intentions. It is her deeds that make her relevant to her society. And there may be no better way of living than to contribute to rather than to take from a person's society. There are cultures that have no statutory welfare. The people who live there seem to have more dignity, and far less anger. Voluntary alms for the poor is one thing. To make it into a "right" has quite different consequences. People who are dependent on others for their existence have a seething hatred for their keepers.

We know that a certain kind of stupidity may be required to be materialistically successful in a money-driven society. But must one *also* be well-mannered? Probably not. But it obscures the trick they are playing on themselves and others. So what makes a life worth living? Certainly not having a larger wide-screen TV or having one more toilet in your house. Just because we are "ordinary" doesn't mean that we have to be like everybody else. It may mean that we have some work to do to deserve a life that is worth living.

+++++

Why do we die? If there were a god, it would probably be a head's-up that one day we won't be here and it will be too late to live, too late to be worthy of being alive. There is a reason why our lives are not a dress rehearsal for our lives. It might be devastating to flunk life twice in a row.

In our culture, we only get one time around at life. In another culture, you might return in a different form until you get it right. The saying (presumably American) is: "*Life's a bitch and then you die.*" You might think that the relative shortness of life and the belief that you can't do it over would be sufficient for trying to get it right the first time. Apparently it is not enough. What would be "enough" to compel us to get it right the first time? Various religious philosophies have tried different ways of belief about this. None seems to be any better than the others at compelling the need to do our lives right. We seem to be far better at inventing ever more novel ways of getting life wrong – judging from the dissatisfaction that is reported and the rage and violence that erupts. Or are rage and violence the symptoms of a deeper (genetic?) need, and peace and love only a human-made utopian myth? Are the majority of people (at least in this modern world) destined to live somewhat perpetually dissatisfied simply because that's the way it is?

+++++

Or is that a condition of modernism? Was there ever a time when people were not so sated with life that they dreamt of some better alternative. Utopias and dystopias have played a part in Western thinking for many years. Personal problems and dissatisfactions have more social currency than do their absence in everyday conversations between and among people. Is this any more than a fashion in our fashion-conscious ways of living in our modern worlds? In *Ethan Frome*, Edith Wharton made an interesting distinction between our "troubles," which elevated one's status, and "complications," which sometimes did us in:

> *"Almost everybody in the neighborhood had 'troubles,' frankly localized and specified; but only the chosen had 'complications.' To have them was in itself a distinction, though it was also, in most cases, a death warrant. People struggled on for years with 'troubles,' but they almost always succumbed to 'complications.'"*

So reporting our personal problems and vague dissatisfactions in the modern world can be seen as the kinds of "troubles" people had in Wharton's time. Having them provided a certain "distinction," a certain status among those one socialized with. What's most interesting here is that one could live on with one's troubles, but that they sometimes led to complications. It is much the same today. One's "troubles" lead to more troubles. A person who has more troubles is likely to have even more troubles. The complication may come from the amassing of troubles and their interactions. What started out as a matter of keeping up with the Joneses could become a condition that led to that death warrant. The pursuit of status by having more troubles than most others could become a pathway to disablement or death – a self-fulfilling prophesy of the worst kind. There are fashions in the troubles people perform in public. Just because they are fashions does not mean that the consequences cannot be quite real, that we might not succumb to the complications they bring to our lives.

+++++

We have the same 24 hours per day that others have. What are we supposed to do with our lives, measured as they are by passing days and years? We know that days misspent are days we can't have back for better purposes. We also know that we spend far more on people who have "troubles" than on people who don't. Some American Indian tribes considered a person's health as a *duty* to the larger tribe. We don't see it that way. Are the consequences different? We seem not to realize that different perspectives lead to different outcomes. We seem not to realize that what we call a thing in life brings with it a perspective that might be good for us, or bad for us. For example, Lillian Hellman wrote (in *The Autumn Garden*):

> *"Lonely people talking to each other can make each other lonelier."*

So what do we do? We warehouse (usually older) lonely people in a place where they have few people to talk to except lonely people. We also are beginning to realize that sick people talking to each other can make each other sicker. So we warehouse them with other people who are sick. We might imagine that our technologies are going to save us from our wrong-headed perspectives. They will not...because they can not.

+++++

Whether or not a life is worth living depends on the person whose life it is, doesn't it? It depends on one's perspective on life. Some despair. So they do away with their lives, considering them not worth living. Others, who have what would seem to us observers worse lives, adapt. They make a life out of a life they didn't choose. Again, it is a very subjective thing – as all lives are, ultimately. Artists may struggle with this. What they are doing is intended to be of value to their larger society. The larger society doesn't always agree. There have been more failures than successes in this calling. Van Gogh despaired of his work. An indifferent public affected him deeply. But he didn't jump off a cliff. Sometimes a person does jump off a cliff when rejected by just one other person. To the person spurned – not getting his or her heart's desire – it may seem like and be played out as a tragedy. But the consequences may be a boon to the larger society. After all, there are plenty of consummated desires that turn out to be a bane to the larger society. Not every coupling is a worthy one from the perspective of the larger whole.

A life worth living is, like truth and beauty, in the eye of the beholder. What to a young person is seen as benevolent may, from the perspective of his or her parent, be seen as malevolent. There is something to the jokes and the stories about in-laws. Poor and oppressed people may not snuff out their own lives at the same rate as well-to-do and privileged people do. On what "objective" basis should a person qualify for assisted suicide? Would you terminate your own life? Would you help a friend who wanted your help to terminate his or her life? By what rationale?

We know from anecdotal evidence and statistically that people who are more engaged in their lives are also likely to be more satisfied with the lives they have. We know that people who have become marginalized (like Van Gogh?) are more likely to do violence to themselves – or to other people. We know that people who devote their lives to a *worthy* purpose of some sort are most likely to contemplate their lives as worth living. We know that the more dependent people are on the largesse of the larger society, the more vindictive they are likely to become. If dissatisfaction with one's life is largely subjective, then satisfaction with one's life must be equally subjective. There are a great many people in this world of ours who are poorer than what we consider poor in our modern society. But they don't seem to perform nearly as much envy or anger about their state of things. Why is that? Human "rights" are not nearly as important in poorer countries as in richer countries? Why is that?

Aristotle said that *"The actuality of thought is life."* That of course is a very philosophical perspective. But is he saying that people who can't think have lesser lives? Is he saying that the possibility of thought is what life is all about? That our concerns with life are a function of the fact that we can think about it, and talk about it? So would that mean that people who can think have better lives than those who can't? If so, then given the fact that most people can't think, would that in itself account for the burgeoning number of people who are at least vaguely dissatisfied with their lives? But wouldn't thinking people therefore be more dissatisfied with their lives than unthinking people? There would be little real evidence to support that. People who are *not* philosophical about their lives seem often to be more satisfied with their lives. Thinking is not a universal good. It may be more a matter of what a person thinks about – and how – and thus the perspectives on life that come from thinking (and talking, its objective counterpart) about what constitutes the "good" life. The "good" life makes sense only compared to a not-good life. Elizabeth Wordsworth wrote (in *Good and Clever):*

> *"If all the good people were clever,*
> *And all clever people were good,*
> *The world would be nicer than ever*
> *We thought that it possibly could."*

This may resonate with Dr. Seuss as well. (A truism seems cleverer in rhyme.) The apposition of "good" and "clever" is useful. For our purposes, it may suggest that there are good people, and then there are clever people, and that clever people are not necessarily good, and that good people are not necessarily clever. Given her time in history, Wordsworth may have been assuming that clever people take advantage of others for their own benefit, and that good people do not. This may seem to us too simplistic. But it might be useful, even so. Do good people, in this sense, have worthier lives than do clever people? Is the fact that good people are good *for* the people they come in contact with a pertinent perspective? Whatever else it may be, a life worth living is one that enriches the lives of others who come into contact with it – aesthetically, intellectually, emotionally, pragmatically, and humanely. This was, as we have seen, the cultural perspective taken by many of the indigenous American Indian tribes. Counter-intuitively, that perspective is that the more a person contributes to the quality of others' lives, the better that person's life will be. This in turn raises the question: Is a life worth living to be had in what one can get from others, or in what that person contributes to the society in which he or she lives? There is plenty of evidence that people who are out to get what they can from life most often impoverish their lives by making this a lifestyle. To care about other people is a matter of refusing to let them default themselves – not indulging them. Goethe admonished: We must love people not for what they *are*, but for what they *could* or should be. This pulls them in the direction of *becoming* that better kind of person, of having a purpose in life. In America, we are all stunted by others' acceptance of who we are, or have been. Even though that is ancient wisdom, there must be many, many modern parents who don't have that perspective even about their own children.

+++++

In his *Endgame,* Samuel Beckett offered us the following exchange to chew on:

> "Clov: Do you believe in the life to come?
> Hamm: Mine was always like that."

Most people have good intentions about the life they are going to have, the life they would have if only they could have. The problem is, most people never get around to implementing those intentions. And as solipsistic as we are, the reason they give is that circumstances external to them made it impossible. Too much to do, too little time. Or they were abused in their early lives, and this is supposed to excuse them. They chose the wrong parents, and kept on choosing the wrong parents the rest of their lives. Many cultures have afterlives, as Christians had theirs in "Heaven." Belief is often an excuse for inaction or changes that need to be made. In the Christian perspective, if one really believes in the life to come, one is morally bound to do what needs doing to make it so in one's lifetime on earth. In the Buddhist perspective, it was a matter of becoming the Buddha, not waiting for him to absolve us. The point is that *putting off* making one's own life worth living was often considered as much of a sin as making a life that isn't worth living. All that in the way of a reminder. In *Our Town,* Thornton Wilder wrote:

> *"Oh, earth, you're too wonderful for anybody to realize you…. Do any human beings ever realize life while they live it? – every, every minute?"*

We take life for granted, until we are sentenced to lose it. "Realizing" life is provocative. We all live our lives – short or long, thwarted or not, in control or out of control, adequately or inadequately – we all live the lives we have. We make of it what we have personally to make of it. We do not and can not control the circumstances that become the context within which we have to make our lives. Our choice is to live life *because of…* or *in spite of.* We will either become what we permit the circumstances to make of us, or what we make of the circumstances. Those are the two generic perspectives on a life worth living – or not. What our lives mean to us is what they mean to us as individual persons. There is no answer to the abstract question "What does living a life mean?" We do not have lives in the abstract. We experience life. How we experience it depends upon who we are. It depends not upon the meanings it imposes on us (which is an exemplary oxymoron), but upon the meaning we impose on it. *[An oxymoron is a statement that is implausible. In this case it is a logical, even an empirical, impossibility.]* That is, the world does not impose its meanings on us. We impose our meanings on it. That's probably close to what Wilder meant by "realizing life."

More reminders: To realize life may require the capability of imposing the kinds of meaning on the world that would enable any of us imposers to live a life worth living. If one's mind is not capable of that, then the fault would lie within us and not in that world. Whatever meaning we have to ourselves, to others, or to the rest of the world comes from us. The world is in no way obligated to be as we say it is. It imposes no meaning on us. All meaning is a function of people, not of the world in which they live. And the human world and all of its artifacts are increasingly our habitat. It is people who have made the worlds in which we live in our minds and with other people and their perspectives, and all of the social artifacts thereto.

+++++

So what does it mean to ponder: What constitutes *a life worth living*? The key word here has to do with *worthiness*. Let us take the perspective that a life worth living is the one that fulfills that person's *worthy* purposes. And what are worthy purposes in life? Aren't they the kind of purposes that are efficacious for the person, but are at the same time efficacious for any person who is affected by them in some way, and thus efficacious for the social groups/societies in which all participate? Who you are and how you perform your life has consequences for the larger society, whether intended or not. You can deny that responsibility. But those whose lives are diminished are affected anyway. In other words, *a life worth living is one that enhances the health and welfare of everyone around you, and the health and welfare of all of those who come along in the wake left by how you lived your life.* A life that does not minimally accomplish this is not a life worth living.

+++++

We all have a life. It has a beginning. It has an ending. No one gets more of it than what is allotted. We all have the same 24 hours in a day, for the days that are our allotment. We are not privy in advance to how many of those days we have. Nor do we have – which television shows and films have – even the possibility of a do-over. Our lives are once, and done, minute by minute, day by day.

What any person makes of the raw material – time and mind – is ultimately a result of the succession of choices that person makes from the beginning to the end. No one else has the mind you have. Thus no one else can be blamed (or credited) with what you become – what you make of your guest appearance here on earth. If you do not make the world you share with others in some way better than it was when you arrived here, you will have failed.

So what is the *test* of a life worth living?

Not failing.

Perspective 14

Playing the Game

There are trivial pursuits. There are serious pursuits. There are time-killing pursuits. There are time-enhancing pursuits. There are engaging pursuits. There are indifferent pursuits. There are internal pursuits (such as the hopes and dreams we might have). And there are external pursuits (such as making the world a better place for others). There are pursuits that you can control. And there are pursuits that get tripped up by the events of the day. Doing life is a project. This makes you a project manager. Some people are competent at this, and some people are not. You do not choose when or where to arrive on this earth. Most do not choose when to depart the worlds in which they live. Most of what just occurs is random. The random events of a life don't care whether you are successful in your pursuits or not. You may try to *will* your pursuits to fruition. But no one cares but you. The world has a say-so in your life. And the world cares little or not at all about what your motives or your passions may be. You make your way in life by making your way in life. If you treat your worlds with indifference, it will pay you back with indifference. If you treat your world as an adversary, it will reciprocate by treating you as an adversary. If you try to do good that requires a change in the status quo, you will meet resistance, probably even be punished in some way. If you try to "conquer" a mountain, you might die in the attempt. Just because you "love" someone doesn't make you good for them. The world is not anyone's friend or accomplice. That's because we don't know how to befriend it. Or ourselves.

Shakespeare suggested that all the world's a stage – and that we are all players on it. We play our roles more or less well, the play proceeds by how we played our roles, and our progeny are stuck with the consequences. Churchill shared this perspective: that a world run by people for people is theater. The fundamental "game" we play is that we are dropped into the play while it is itself being improvised by the players extant. We take up or fall into one or more of the roles available. We follow the script as best we can. The script keeps changing because it is constantly evolving as a result of how the billions of people involved interpret the story they imagine they are in and play their roles as they are channeled (both inwardly and outwardly) to do so. The game of human life evolves as it is being played.

The games of life are not ours to control. No person can. What happens in Timbuktu can have consequences for us. It may be so small as to be imperceptible. But it changes the game. If we don't adapt, we begin losing the game. We may think we can beat the game. But we can't. If we don't adapt, if we don't know how to play the game as it is constantly changing, we have "folded." We can drop out of the game. But it will still be going on as it was before we were born and will be after we have departed. The game being played will influence our lives whether we are active participants or not. If we are sentient, we are in the game, whether actively or passively or indiscriminately. The game will go on, with or without us. We are not the measure of the game. The game is a measure of us.

Every casual – or not so casual – conversation is a game. Every organization amongst other organizations is involved in a game. Marriage is a game, just as friendship is a game. Adultery is an obvious game. Children game the world they live in. Adults are gamed by the world they live in. Teachers game their pupils just like bankers game their customers. People who have something to sell game the people who might want to buy. Buyers game the world of suppliers. Nations game one another. Life games us. The challenge is to game life. No one ever gets out of life alive. It is the arenas in which the games are played that live on. Those arenas in which the game is played change, as do the rules of the game. Those who do not or cannot play the games being played...lose. If you don't know how to win at playing the game of an extramarital affair, you lose. If you are taught or otherwise learn how to be a loser, it's likely you will be a loser. If you are taught or otherwise learn how to be a winner at the game of life, you will be up against others who may be able to play the game better than you do. For the most part, it is a competitive game that we play, even though our competitors may be invisible to us. You can guess. But you can never know even what your spouse is thinking. The outcome is always in the future.

In *The Will to Power,* Nietzsche said:

> *"Fundamental thought: we must consider the future as decisive for all our evaluations – and not seek the laws of our action behind us!"*

Fundamental, indeed! No matter how clever our strategies, the outcomes of the games we play today are in the future. We like to imagine that experience is the best teacher. But the games of life we are playing today didn't occur yesterday. The games of life we are playing today can be judged only by their outcomes, not by the laws of action that seemed to work yesterday. Success or failure can only be judged by how things turn out. No theory, no method, no belief can be any better than its consequences. We moderns tend to think that a plan based on the methods of some past success will win the game. We would be wrong on two counts:

1. The "laws" of the actions we take can be deduced only from the present circumstances. The world today is not what it was yesterday. And you are not the person you were yesterday – and neither is anyone else.

2. The second is even more intriguing. We moderns are very susceptible to the notion that if we had an achievement in the

past, that would be due to us. The "ism" at work here is that of radical individualism. We are prone to believe that we are individually to be credited with any successes we may have had, but that any failures were due to other factors. So we think of our perspectives on life and work and love to be proprietary, and therefore superior.

People who attribute their successes in life to themselves are leaving out the primary player in all games. And that is *luck*. The world (us included) is rarely as rational as our methods are likely to be. Things are more irrational (i.e., random) than we give them credit for. In the fourth century B.C., the influential playwright Euripides offered this observation in *The Heracleidae*:

> *"In this world the lucky person passes for a genius."*

How often have you seen people rising to celebrity-hood on the basis of, really, luck? We want to canonize the person who is presumed to have been accountable for some notable success. In doing so, we overlook the many other variables at work in the game being played, the key variable always being…luck. It isn't that hard work and better thinking don't matter. They do. But they are merely ante for getting into the game. The game people play will turn out the way they do. But attributing that to happenstance or simply good luck is far more accurate than attributing it to one individual's actions. Steve Jobs was certainly smart. But in the game of business there are too many working parts to attribute the outcome to the actions of one individual. Nor is it the case that luck is "smarter" than the person we want to attribute it to. In any complex game, the forces at work go way beyond the actions of any one individual, no matter her actions or her faith or her position.

> *"Leaders" do not make their organizations successful. Their organizations make them successful – or not.*

Our pop culture perspectives and the biases of our peculiar grammar (of life) make this hard to believe. But to fail to take action in that direction leaves us with insoluble problems. In his *Maxims* (17th-century), La Rochefoucauld offered a useful perspective on this dilemma:

> *"Fortunate people seldom mend their ways, for when good luck crowns their misdeeds with success they think it is because they are right."*

To hold people "accountable" in a complex system that they do not – can not – control, is the central flaw in rationality. And its symptoms appear every day, causing us problems where there are none, and perhaps causing us to miss the problems that really do exist. For example, a whole industry has grown up around the *symptoms* of problems. Vaccinating large numbers of people against the possibility of contracting certain prevalent diseases has been an exception. But we know precious little about predicting organ failure. We know (reluctantly, at the time) that better sanitation played a larger role in saving lives than did the medicine of the day. But we know precious little about the psychosocial factors that precede some of the degenerative conditions – like depression or drug addiction. That's because the dominant perspective of modern medicine is curing diseases and not preventing them. (As an aside, there's not much money to be made from obviating psychosocial problems at their source, much money to be made from treating their symptoms... so those psychosocial problems continue to multiply.)

"Accountability" is a fashionable term in modern management circles. But most people do not intend to fail on purpose. Failure is as complex and non-reducible as is success. Yet if our perspective is to single out someone to blame for success, we are inclined to single out someone to blame for some problem that just occurs. Success sometimes just occurs. The real problem may be in our perspective and not the outcomes – which may have multiple contributions, even from randomness.

Stanislaw Lec (yes, the snowflake in an avalanche guy) gave us something to ponder in his inimitable way when he asked:

> *"If a man who cannot count finds a four-leaf clover, is he lucky?"*

There are many useful ways of interpreting this. One is that being able to count is a prerequisite for feeling lucky if you find a four-leaf clover. If a person can't count, how could he consider himself "lucky" if he found a four-leaf clover? If a person wins the lottery from a ticket he found in the trash, is he lucky? Using their subjective theories about how to pick a winning ticket, are the five million or so other people just unlucky? Or, because of our cultural perspectives, does the anomaly get publicized and the many losers it takes to make a winner get overlooked? If your car is crashed into by another driver, does that make you accountable? What were you doing on that street at that moment anyway?

We can explain anything. The explanation may have nothing to do with what actually happened. The columnist Evan Esar may have touched upon this when he wrote: *"It's the good luck of other people that makes us dissatisfied with our own."* Is there something psychological about our belief in luck? Is there something social about how we feel about it? Luck seems to be something we can't explain unless we believe we are either lucky or unlucky. And then that becomes our explanation. Does the explanation game have anything to do with how randomly events may occur?

+++++

If people go to "see" the doctor, or sign up for graduate school or long-term financial advice or for insurance, they are entering into a game. If you go out to "buy" a car, there might be as many as ten different people having ten different perspectives (or agendas) involved. Does this put you in control of the situation or its outcome? Are you accountable for the choice you made, or was the loan officer or the commercial you saw on television?

If you wanted to "see" the doctor, you could have made a video of her the first time you were there. Euphemisms abound. When we are playing the game of lust, we often refer to it as "love." We don't ask "Where is the toilet?" We ask, "Where is the restroom?" Are we really going there to rest? Professional football players don't get into that game because they can make a lot of money. They do it for their love of the game. The boss doesn't fire someone just because they are stupid, incompetent or just plain lazy. People lie on their applicant bios. If asked (not very often) why, they might reply "Because the company lied to me." Or that "Everyone does it." Women call it make-up. But they don't necessarily tell you what game they are making-up for. The more money a male makes, the more perks he is likely to have in the games he plays. We call it higher education. But what most people are there for are the credentials they have been told will gain them a fatter paycheck.

We are influenced by certain people in certain ways all of our lives. It is from them that we learn what we are supposed to call things, how we are to explain things. Useful or not, pertinent or not, beneficial or not, this is the raw material used when we somewhat euphemistically refer to making up our own minds about something – making a choice or a decision about what is going on and what we should do about it. The perspectives we don't import from other sources are perspectives we are not likely to have. And yet it is our perspectives that channel what we pay attention to, what things mean to us and what we mean to them, and most of the actions we take. We imbibe our worlds according to the perspectives we impose upon them. We think of ourselves according to the perspectives we have for doing so. Our lives hinge upon the perspectives we have devised (or that have been devised for us) for doing so. Our lives unfold in the perspectives we deploy, whatever their source may have been.

+++++

It is not commonplace to think of – to have the perspective of looking at – life as a game. We have our psychological and cultural myths about how to conduct our lives. They do not exist as a benefit to us. They exist because they are consistent with the theories and beliefs in which people have a vested interest. A vested interest in how we think about things, how we perceive things, comes from repeated use over time. As we have seen, it doesn't matter if those perspectives work for our benefit or against our benefit. The more we use them, the more habituated we become to them. We have a vested interest in what we believe simply because it is we who see the world that way. We are who we are because we see our world the way we see it. And who we are is resistant to any change – even if it is a change for the better.

To the making of metaphors about what life *is*, there seems to be no limit. In modern times, there is even more free-wheeling. There is a popular song lyric that offers the metaphorical proposition that "Life is just a bowl of cherries...." It may be difficult to make that literal – what could that mean, literally? Still, the making of metaphors about what life *is* beyond the medical perspective may be all we have. The only "truths" we humans have are human truths. The best medical or scientific perspective is still a metaphor. Vital signs are not evidence of any life we are experiencing. It just portends that we haven't died yet. Physicians do not live their lives literally. They live their lives just like the rest of us – metaphorically. As the famous physicist and Nobel laurate Richard Feynman was quoted as saying:

> *"Physics is like sex. It may give some practical results, but that's not why we do it."*

Why *do* we do it? Why do we do anything? Because our perspectives, whatever their source, tell us to? So the perspective that life is a game that we people play is not to displace all the other metaphors. It is to suggest that the "game" metaphor may have some healthy benefits that other metaphors don't have.

So what is it that makes life game-like? It is the same thing that makes any competitive game so compelling. It is that we can never know for sure what the other person or persons are thinking. In the same way that we have no access to the poker adversary's cards, we have no access to any adversary's mind. The pugilist can only guess what his opponent is thinking when she feints the way she does. Lovers can be very intimate about some things. But you can never know what the other person is thinking. You can only guess. "Falling" in love is apt, because we can never know how it is going to turn out. We like certainty. We try to make it more certain by making the bond a sacred one, or at least a legal one. But for reasons only the perpetrator can know, spouses have been known to murder their counterparts throughout history. Betrayal makes the game more exciting, even if not necessarily to one's liking. We like certainty. But when we watch television dramas, it is the indeterminacy of things that grabs us. We watch sports on television because we don't (can't) know how the game is going to turn out.

To fall in love is to enter a world in which another person plays a key role. We can know what we think, but we cannot know what the other person thinks. Falling in love is exciting. The mundane everyday life that often follows is not. The falling in love game seems somehow to be displaced by the games that start being played when that game is no longer the game being played. At least according to the most popular versions of life after the honeymoon is over, adversarial bickering begins. Sometimes (as in *The War of the Roses)* disagreements (another game) take over unless the pair agree to some other kind of game.

When you interview for a job, you are playing a role in a game. You cannot know what the interviewer's agenda may be. You can only guess. The interviewer cannot know what your agenda is. He or she can only guess. Sometimes it turns out well. But a lot depends upon how well you play the game. What is this game about? Are there better than conventional ways of playing it?

Parenting is a game. Young children can play the game as well as and often better than the parent can. The person who makes the rules usually has the advantage. And young children learn early on about making the rules, about setting the field of play. Taking the perspective that these are games that people play, and that you have merely been drawn into them, can be beneficial to all sides. As we have seen, being a patient in a doctor's office is very game-like. You are the dependent variable, and the doctor is the independent variable. But it is usually played on her turf and by her rules. Also, as we have seen, if you are a customer of a large corporation, they will revert to their "policy" if there is some disagreement about what is happening. You are not expected to have a policy. If someone crashes into you on the highway, that's one kind of game. If you smash into the sheriff's vehicle, that will turn out to be quite a different kind of game.

The games of life don't have to have winners and losers. They can result in all winners or all losers. Where lovers or partners or friends are concerned, you both lose if an argument turns adversarial. There are dialogs and then there are alternate monologues. In a dialog, both parties win. Where they devolve into alternate monologues, both lose. Where it makes no difference who wins and who loses, the chances that both win are greatly increased.

It all comes down to what is to be accomplished. Where two or more people *abandon* themselves to what they collectively want – or need – to accomplish, there can be no winners or losers. What happens when there is not a result that requires collaboration is that arguments erupt about things that have no real pertinence. We all want to editorialize. That's ego's way. If what's important is what happened a week ago, the focus – or the perspective – is off the present and onto the past. To argue about the rules of a love affair will likely extinguish the desire. When the rules become more important than the accomplishment, it turns all attention to the rules.

What's really important is the perspective that people bring to the situation – whether that is a casual conversation or voting for our lawmakers. In our modern world, a person can be vociferously for or against something without knowing much of anything about that something. This was not always the case in the past, or even in some contemporary civilizations. To recognize that all human encounters are political in nature is advantageous. They are political simply because what person A tells you about person C is rarely ever what person A says directly to person C. They are political simply because what person A tells you about herself is rarely ever what she tells herself about herself. Who you "are" depends more upon who you're talking to – who your auditors are – than it does on who you "are." Our personas change depending upon who our auditors are. Most people never talk to themselves the way they talk to other people. (If they did, they would risk being locked up.) So in the simplest two-person conversation, there are actually at least four persons involved. That's what makes all human encounters (small-p) political in nature.

+++++

That's the micro part of it. The macro part of it is that the context in which you have to play the game is created by the other seven billion people on this earth. The field of play and the rules of the game are created by people other than you. You are not the one who controls the ever-changing circumstances of your life. To alert us to the fact that we may be no more than bit-players or even bystanders in the stories that millions of others are pursuing, oblivious to any interests we may have, the satirist Samuel Butler wrote as follows:

> *"We are like billiard balls in a game played by unskillful players, continually being nearly sent into a pocket, but hardly ever getting right into one, except by a fluke."*

The game we have to perform in is created by millions of others playing their games with no concern for us at all. We arrive in that ongoing, ever-changing game of life while it is in process. The world we live in was not rationally created the day we were born. It has been evolving for the thousands of years that there have been people playing games with one another and themselves. Not by choice, but we inherited the world we live in. We have to play the game with the circumstances dealt to us. We have to play the games that are being played in our social world as we know it. We do not choose our lives. We have to forge our lives within the conditions that are created by millions of others we do not know, and who are pursuing their own agendas. In other words, we get to choose our lives, but only within the parameters and paradigms available to us in our lifetimes. The columnist Evan Esar gave us something useful to ponder:

"A well-adjusted person is one who can play golf
and bridge as if they were games."

And the poorly adjusted person is one who can play the games of life required *as if* they weren't games? Life is, after all, an *as if* business. Malcolm Forbes referred to it as *The Business of Life*. That is a perspective that can be taken. We can play at life as if it had something to do (metaphorically, as in business) with Return on Investment (ROI), and as if there were gains and losses that are supposed to add up to some desired degree of profit from being alive. We could make alliances, buy and sell our time, and even have strategies for achieving the ends sought in being alive. Almost any kind of metaphor works, and provides a provocative, if not useful, perspective. Even so, if you think of life as a zero-sum game, you will not have a rich life. The metaphor will lead you down a dead-end path. And those who prefer the games they can buy to the games that they could live are not always "well-adjusted."

+++++

So we come round once again to the matter of perspective. Our lives are composed of the perspective we impose on the worlds in which we have our lives. The moral of the Adam and Eve parable is obvious but elusive. They lived in what was presumed to be "Paradise." But when they started thinking about, they wondered if there was a somewhere else that they should know about – not unlike our current search for life elsewhere in the universe. In the process of seeking knowledge of their circumstances, they were banished from their Paradise. What is this supposed to mean? That "Curiosity killed the cat?" That seeking knowledge beyond the stewardship of themselves in the place and under the conditions they were given comes of evil? That to pursue the "truth" of everything leads to the loss of what really matters? That even wondering if there is somewhere or something better leads to the loss of what you had before you started wondering? That our species' hubris leads us to believe that whatever our technologies make of us is okay? That we don't have to be knowledge producers or consumers to be happy – to live a good life along the lines that Scott and Helen Nearing chose?

The Japanese novelist Soseki Natsume was a transitional writer bridging the traditional and the modern. One of his aphorisms is as follows:

> *"If you use your knowledge, you will offend. If you ride your emotions, you will be swept away. If you insist on having your way, you will feel cramped. In any case, it is hard to live in this world."*

The average American today might respond "Yeah, tell me about it." It can be hard to live in this world. When our gods (whom we created) banished us from the Garden of Eden, we banished them from their panoply. Now we are free to create our own problems, and to try to solve them with the same mentality with which we created them (difficult if not impossible, as Einstein said). We live in our sometimes hellish world, trying to accumulate enough money to escape it. We are indeed creatures of our own making. We create our worlds to try to escape the responsibility. It hasn't worked yet.

People inherit their basic perspectives from the past and from present pop culture, then create their own perspectives out of those. They do not necessarily lead us into the lives we would like to have. In fact, the very perspectives we impose upon our worlds 24/7 may make it impossible to have the lives we would like to have. One perspective: We are idiots. We are led by idiots. We have been preceded by idiots. What could we expect?

The British renegade thinker Walter Landor was as insightful as he was volatile. He wrote, for example:

> *"Goodness does not more certainly make [people] happy than happiness makes them good."*

Like all great aphorists, Landor expected that this could be interpreted according to his reader's perspectives. One perspective leads you to see it in one way. Another perspective leads you to see it in a different way. For example: happy people are not necessarily good people. And good people are not necessarily happy. There may be a correlation in some cases. But they are not mutually causative in any case. What does it mean to be "good"? That is, what is a person's perspective on the source and the destiny of goodness? Happiness can make you feel good in certain instances. But it won't make you any better or more competent as a human being in an interconnected world. Navy Seals may feel good about killing the bad guys. But does doing so make them "happy"? Both conditions are human concepts, perspective made by people, for people. Doing drugs may make a person feel happy. But an overdose that ends in death cannot. Falling in love may provide you with the delusion of goodness. But if you mistreat one another, it's no longer good. States of existence that have no more than human meaning do not follow the rules of physics. They are ephemeral. They exist only so long as they exist.

From the *Journal* of the Swiss thinker Henri Amiel we have this:

> *"We are never more discontented with others than*
> *when we are discontented with ourselves."*

+++++

Amiel may be trying to lead us to think about two critical perspectives:

1. That it is the games we play with ourselves that provide the feelings we have when we are playing some game with others; and

2. That the feelings we have about others have more to do with the feelings we have about ourselves than about the games we are playing or the people involved.

This is old wisdom, of course. The earliest novels in the East had this as a theme: that our perspectives about others or about what is going on originate in the perspectives we have come to impose on ourselves. We compose others and what happens in the world according to how we see ourselves. These are sometimes referred to as brain-loops. But they are not a function of our brains. They are a function of how we emerge as persons in the interconnectedness of our social lives – that is, how we come to be as synchronized as we are with the others with whom we are playing social games. You can't play a game like a conversation or the stock market unless you are in synch with what these games are and how they are played. You can't engage in a duel unless the other person shows up. You can't be who you are unless there are others who minimally share that perspective with you. They can't be who they are at the time unless you see them in the perspective of the game you are sharing. The intricacies of social life that hold us all loosely in their grip are the perspectives we bring to bear on ourselves and the rest of the world. When those become dysfunctional, personal, interpersonal, and social problems emerge. There are cultural perspectives. When those become dysfunctional, the culture itself begins to fail (as Jared Diamond provides historical evidence). There are sub-cultural perspectives. When social groupings (e.g., epistemic communities) become dysfunctional social pathologies begin to rise. There are personal perspectives. When those become dysfunctional, psychopathologies begin to rise. We can observe this happening in our time. The mental health of the individual depends upon that individual's perspectives on herself and the rest of the world. The health of a culture depends upon its basic perspectives on people and their worlds.

Our perspectives can be efficacious. Our perspectives can be deleterious.

+++++

Our perspectives produce what we take to be reality. They have an insidious capacity for creating the worlds we inhabit – both personal and social. For example, some people suffer bouts of boredom. They attribute this to their "fact" that the world is boring, and that the people they know are boring. Some people are depressed. They see the world as a depressing place. Still other people are deranged. They see the world as a deranged place. Some people are happy. They see the world as a happy place (even though unhappy people see *them* as crazy). Some people are liberal-minded. When the world they live in does not seem as liberal as they need it to be, they set about to fix it according to their perspectives – the way it *should* be. And so on.

We create our worlds in the image of our common or idiosyncratic perspectives on them. This is the "self-fulfilling prophecy" at large. How we see the world we inhabit eventually becomes the world we inhabit – internally and externally. Our world becomes a refraction of the perspectives by which we navigate it. American Indian perspectives on the world they inhabited (at one time the "same" world we inhabited) were radically different from the world modern people inhabit. The worlds we live in are either what we say they are – or they will be remodeled to be so. Our reality is borne in our perspectives about it. Not the other way around.

+++++

Just as in the art world, our perspectives change. One aspect that remains the same is that we don't see the social world in terms of games that have to be played. We are almost never aware of the games we play with ourselves. Because our perspectives used over and over create our "reality," we just take what happens in our lives for granted. At the end of life, most people do not so much regret what they did. They regret what they didn't do. For example, there are these lines from T. S. Eliot's "Burnt Norton":

> *"Footfalls echo in the memory*
> *Down the passage which we did not take*
> *Towards the door we never opened*
> *Into the rose-garden."*

He's saying (among other possibilities) that our perspectives on who we may be are stronger than the perspectives we have on who or what we should or could be. How we perceive ourselves, given our imagined pasts, are like chains that bind us to the way we are. We see ourselves as having an identity (or a "self) that inhibits our becoming even what we desire to be.

We have learned how to play the games we play with others. We have trepidations about playing other games. In the film, *Humoresque,* Oscar Levant ad-libbed:

> *"It is not what you are; it's what you don't become*
> *that hurts."*

This regret was echoed later by Woody Allen, talking about himself in his *Getting Even:*

> *"His one regret in life is that he is not someone*
> *else."*

We envy others. We worship our celebrities. We feel sorry for ourselves. It is all a matter of perspective. The remedy for living was offered by the slave-turned-philosopher Epictetus, when he wrote:

> *"First, say to yourself what you would be; then do*
> *what you have to do."*

The problem is that our collective perspectives over time have incapacitated us. Most thoroughly modern people are incapable of doing either one with the degree of commitment and competence required. They can't disentangle themselves from the perspectives that subordinate the future to the past.

+++++

If you are reading a book, you are likely using your own perspectives to do so. What it means comes from you, not the material you are reading. It is your interpretation that you are getting. The better at subordinating yourself to new and more efficacious perspectives, what Eliot called the passage you do not take, the more life you will have in living. It is the same for yourself and the perspectives that could lift you out of the cave you are in. To have a better life, you have to have better perspectives on how to play the game of de-centering yourself.

Our perspectives on the game of aging speed the process of aging, e.g. –

> *"A person is not old until regrets take the place of hopes and plans."*
>
> --Scott Nearing

Perspective 15

On Knowing vs. Doing

Yes, you "know" what Epictetus said. But the distance between knowing and doing is the longest distance there is for most people. What you merely know will not equip you to do anything but talk to other people who know about the same things. When the early Greeks separated the knower from the known, they created the commodity we now perceive as "knowledge." It was a paradigm shift having huge consequences. You can buy knowledge. But you cannot buy the competence to use it. In ancient times, the knower and what he or she knew were two aspects of the same thing. Not in today's world. Making knowledge into a commodity led to a world in which, if you think you want or need the knowledge that someone owns (like teachers, financial "experts," computer technicians, tabloid publishers, etc.) you have to buy it. When you have sufficient knowledge (or the assumed credentials thereto), you can charge others for your knowledge, whether you are a professor, an IT tech, or a home decorating advisor. You may be able to buy the knowledge you imagine you want, or to sell the proprietary knowledge you have acquired. It is only in a world in which knowledge can be bought and sold that there are people who are considered to be experts. When what was known was freely provided if asked (as in farming communities of the past), some people had the knowledge that others needed, and some people were in need of the knowledge others had (got mainly by experience).

Those are two different worlds. The lingering Amish of today opted out of the federal insurance plan for universal health care. Their rationale? They felt they didn't need to pay for insurance because they provided for one another in their communities. If someone got sick, others were there to help. If they needed other kinds of help, there were others who were ready and willing to provide it. They didn't comprehend paying for knowledge because they believed that it should be shared freely, much as their other needs were warranted by the community in advance. Even though Americans spend more for medical advice than any other nation, we rank near the middle of all nations in terms of health.

The educational model that has taken over is one that is devoted almost exclusively to knowing-about. If you want to know how, you have to pay for that separately, or depend upon your own or your immediate peers' experiences to learn how. Since most parents these days don't really know much about parenting – because their own parents didn't – they have to get that knowledge by paying for it.

Primarily because there is money to be made by providing the advice people want or need, and because no guarantees are included, there are charlatans at work. So the advice you buy may be good for you or bad for you. It depends upon how cleverly and appealingly it was promoted, by the media or word of mouth. If you trust your friends, you will buy what they promote. If you trust the media source, you will buy what they promote. The advice (or the "information") you buy will never be any better than you are at discriminating the good for you from the bad for you. It seems that the pharmaceutical business paid almost twice as much for lobbying than did the cigarette manufacturers. You might wonder whether or not their getting rich on the stuff or the knowledge you buy will be any healthier for you in the long run than what the cigarette manufacturers proffered. When you solicit knowledge from your friends or acquaintances, will it be your agenda or theirs that is being served? When you take advice indirectly from your celebrities, is it your agenda or their agenda that is being served? *It is only the sources that you trust that can betray you.* When you go to school (at any level), are you taught to know when and how to trust? Knowing-about won't help you in such situations. You need to know *how*. In *De officiis*, Cicero (1st-century B.C.) warned:

> *"Knowledge of the universe would somehow*
> *be. . .defective were no practical results to follow."*

True, Cicero lived in a much more pragmatic age. And he may have been more pragmatic than our present-day philosopher-kings seem to be. But most school-age children know more *about* the universe than they do about their own teachers or parents...or even about themselves and their lives. Or about what's required to pursue a good life on this planet.

"Defective" is fairly strong condemnation. Of course we can't know what Cicero (or his translator) meant by using this term. Cicero neither spoke nor wrote in English. But he seems to be saying that *some* knowledge had some practical value and that other knowledge took us in the direction of knowledge for knowledge's sake and not in the direction of its practical value. By this we know that knowledge that did not have some practical value for making a good life (fundamental to the Romans and the Greeks) was not only useless, but potentially detrimental. It remains the case. If what you know fills your mind with intellectual trivia which you have no need to know, it crowds out the knowledge that you need for living a good life. The present discontent with one's life in spite of the tsunami of "information" we are exposed to every day may be a symptom of this immorality: of being filled up with knowledge that has no practical value to you or to the destiny of your society. People may be able to talk more and more about stuff that doesn't really matter. But they are less good at life-making than perhaps their predecessors were. Morality has to do with what is efficacious for persons and for their societies. Separating this from knowledge in order to make knowledge into a commodity has, and continues to have, its ill effects. *Talk is not neutral. It is either efficacious in its consequences for the people involved and their societies, or it is not.* In the context of his other writings, this is probably what Cicero meant.

+++++

To know a thing or a person in one way is an impediment to knowing that person or that thing in another way. What we sometimes refer to as resistance to change is the mechanism involved. We change very slowly, and over time, because once we know what's what and who's who, we are not looking for alternatives. Adults are not good learners because they already know what they think they need to know to get by for the rest of their lives. They are in general not very susceptible to learning a different way of looking at things. And therein lies the central function of *perspective*. It is a more or less habitual way of comprehending what goes on in one's world. And habits of comprehending the world in one way resist any outside or inside attempt made to comprehend it in some different (or especially some contradictory) way.

What we know sets us on a course of fulfilling how we know that thing. We name it. We are good at seeing the world as we know it. We seek confirmation of what we know. If we happen upon disconfirmation of what we already know, we become experts at avoiding or dismissing it. We are on a mission. And that mission is to be right, even though other people have to be wrong for us to be right. We go where our knowledge (our perspective on things) lead us. It is anathema to us to be wrong. So we assume we are right. We see the world as we know it. And we must be right because it is we who know it. The "practical results" of what we know come from what we know. There is no "truth" involved. The only measure we have of whether what we know is what we *need to know* is the practical results that come of that knowledge. If it doesn't take us where we ought to be going, it will take us where we ought not to be going.

+++++

In *The Passionate State of Mind: And Other Aphorisms*, Eric Hoffer offered yet another perspective on knowing that is crucial to our understanding:

> *"Far more crucial than what we know or do not know is what we do not want to know."*

What we "do not *need* to know" may have put a better point on it. We may "want" to know many things we have no need to know. People who do not know what they need to know have a mind like a junkyard for "information." Closely related is the anonymous saying: *"You can never know too little of what is not worthy knowing at all."* This is somewhat cryptic. But what's behind such a folk saying is this: Our capacity for knowing is finite. What's available has become (thanks to the technologies involved) almost infinite. We are so overburdened with information (what used to be called knowledge, but is no longer) that we have lost sight of what it may all mean. If you know what you need to know, and collect only that, you will have a much better handle on what it means for you and for your life.

In his "Words and Reality," T. H. Huxley warned us:

> *"…knowledge is dependent upon being; as we are,*
> *so we know."*

Isn't Huxley saying that who we are and what we know are two aspects of the same thing? You are who you are because you know what you know. And you know what you know because you are who you are. Both who you are and what you know (or even seek to know) are perspectival – that is, you have certain perspectives on the world because of who you are and what you know. These will channel your thinking, your feelings, and your performance in the world. Others don't see you in terms of who you "are" and what you know. All they have to go on is your performance in their presence. To them, you are who you are because you perform what you know, and you perform what you know because you are who you are…to them. The birds and the bees know a lot. They just don't talk about what they know. They just play their roles without questioning them or reflecting upon them. We talk about what we presume we know. No other critters do that. It is at once our presumed superiority, but most of our problems are created there.

The British author Frederic Harrison offered this useful aphorism:

"Man's business here is to know for the sake of living, not to live for the sake of knowing."

Whatever best serves the lives we ought to be living is worth knowing. What is not may not be worth knowing. To know what is worth knowing requires an understanding of the lives we ought to be living. That insight, long averred as wisdom, has to come first. It gets lost in the maelstrom of the information we expose ourselves to in this modern world. We value knowledge as a commodity. But we have lost sight of why we wanted it in the first place. The poet E. E. Cummings offered yet another valuable perspective on knowing-about when he wrote:

"Knowledge is a polite word for dead but not buried imagination."

Ideas are born in imagination. By the time those ideas and their progeny become knowledge, they are already dead – just not yet buried. The difference between knowledge and wisdom is that knowledge goes out of date. Wisdom never does. Contrary to popular opinion, knowledge does not produce wisdom. It is not the source of wisdom. It is not the precursor of wisdom. It may even be a modern excuse for wisdom. We harbor the belief that knowledge is truth, and that if we have enough of it, we will finally arrive at the ultimate truth of things. A useful truth about things is that knowledge is a commodity. It is bought and sold every day in this world of ours. Is that why we are here – to accumulate knowledge as if there were no better way of living?

+++++

You may know about lots of stuff. But the knowledge you imbibe does not come with a guarantee that it is correct. Mark Twain is quoted as quipping:

"It ain't what you don't know that gets you into trouble. It's what you know for sure that just ain't so."

People are usually pretty sure of what they know. It's a bit like believing that the detergent you use is the best. It's the best because why would you use it if it weren't the best. After all, your taste is impeccable. But, as Twain warned us, it isn't so much what we don't know that gets us into trouble (although that happens frequently), it's what we know for sure that just isn't so. Back in the days (not so long ago) when the controversy was brewing about whether the earth was flat or round, most people could muster evidence that their point of view (or perspective) was correct and the opposite point of view was wrong. Ships that went to sea would likely fall off the edge. Even some maps showed this to be so. If you married someone your mother didn't approve of, it sometimes turned out that she was right and your illusions were wrong. H. L. Mencken, whose evidence for his ability to resist temptation was that he didn't start smoking cigars until he was nine years old, had nonetheless an acerbic and ranging wit, to wit:

> *"For every complex problem there is an answer*
> *that is clear, simple, and wrong."*

All problems are solvable by those who purport to have the knowledge to solve them, and that would be most people most of the time. We may have more solutions than problems, with certain perennial problems hanging around because our answers were wrong. Since it is impossible to predict the future with any reliability (ask the stock-market pundits), no one can really predict how your love affair is going to turn out – especially you. We like to believe that our knowledge will permit us to see everything for what it is, and to understand everything. That our accumulated knowledge over many years does not thus aggrandize us is one of those complex problems that has answer after answer, each one successively clear, simple, and wrong. Alexander Pope was trying to be helpful to us hubristic humans when he wrote:

> *"Some people will never learn anything for this*
> *reason, because they understand everything too*
> *soon."*

It is better to know the questions that need asking than to know all of the answers. In a culture where status comes from knowing rather than curiosity, and where education is based on knowing the answers, most young people understand things too soon. As a result, they fall out of the learning mode and into the purgatory of the knowing mode. Learning begins when you don't have the answers. And, as a reminder, *Learning = Growth, and Growth = Life*. People who are not in the learning mode all of their lives thus fail to grow in their lives. Those who know only the answers forfeit a significant part of their lives for their certainty. Madame de Souvre, Marquise de Sable, famed among the highest-ranking intellectuals of her day, offered a similar perspective:

> *"Often the desire to appear competent impedes our ability to become competent, because we are more anxious to display our knowledge than to learn what we do not know."*

What we know is miniscule compared to what we do not know. It is a sort of refusal to grow up. We want to be forever young when we knew it all. What she adds to this perspective is that wanting to appear competent gets in the way of our becoming competent. One can only become more competent by asking questions – not by making statements, especially if those statements are corroborated by the others you hang out with. If what you can learn by asking doesn't make you more competent in your roles in life, you're not asking the right questions. Life requires doing, not just knowing. If you can't do good with what you know, it's clutter – junk. Madame de Sable is also saying, by how she lived her life, that it makes a great deal of difference who you hang out with. If you hang out with incompetent people, you won't learn much of value, nor will you grow much as a person.

+++++

Einstein famously asserted:

> *"Imagination is more important than knowledge."*

A paradoxical kind of comment coming from a scientist/ mathematician and someone who changed our perspective on the world we inhabit. Was it solely for him he was talking about? Or did he intend people in general? Let's go with the latter, because it was probably what he meant as the statement is taken in context.

Einstein believed, along with many other scientists, that *"as our circle of knowledge expands, so does the circumference of darkness surrounding it."* In other words, what we don't know (or can't know) expands at a faster rate than does what we assume we do know. It takes imagination to penetrate what it is we do not know. Knowledge itself doesn't *do* anything but accumulate. It takes people of imagination to ask questions about what we do not know – both personally and collectively. It is questions – curiosity, really – that accounts for progress. Knowledge is a static noun, not an active verb. It doesn't *do* anything. Only people can do things with their knowledge. Or, like Edison, if they don't have it, with their questions, with their imagination and their determination to achieve an outcome. As the French artist Francis Picabia believed, evidenced by his own life:

+++++

"Knowledge is ancient error reflecting on its youth."

Add to this the saying that *"Youth is a defect that corrects itself with time.* Taken together, the metaphor speaks volumes to our perspective here.

Knowledge is always past tense. It is ancient "error" because subsequent knowledge has always corrected it. It is a perspective on how youthful exuberance turns into taciturnity with the seasoning of hindsight. It's an ancient error because all knowledge is provisional, never final. Those who tout their knowledge are clinging to what is presently known – by them. The pretense of certainty defies the history of ideas. That is, more subtly, what Einstein meant by asserting that imagination is more important than facts. Facts are dead things. The reach of the imagination is a living thing.

Does this mean that wisdom itself is provisional? Knowledge is not wisdom. Wisdom is not a commodity. It is not even communicable. It is something that is achieved by a person, not something that can be bought or sold in a marketplace. People who are trying to buy wisdom are wasting their money. What people are capable of learning is a function of that person, not of what there is to be learned. Most people think that they are capable of knowing whatever there is to be known. But most people are not capable. No one is capable of understanding what *they* are not individually capable of understanding. It was Heraclitus who said:

"Much learning does not teach understanding."

If he were around today in our modern world, where going to school to learn the answers to all of the questions on the paper-and-pencil test does not lead to understanding but the process of attempting to transfer knowledge to one's charges seems actually to diminish the possibilities of their understanding. Stupidity rises when so much knowledge is on sale or is even "free." Knowledge has very little to do with understanding.

+++++

The *doing* part of what seems otherwise a conundrum is intriguing. The Chinese saying is as follows:

"I hear and I forget;
I see and I remember;
I do and I understand."

I *do* and I understand. Where knowledge is perceived as a commodity (as in Western cultures), we are led to believe that it can be "transferred" from one person to another by telling. What we see around us when we observe other people is something that may or may not impact some people. But if we really want to understand something, we have to do it. Then we *begin* to understand. In our own past history, it was Aristotle who said:

"What we learn to do, we learn by doing."

You can read an instruction manual about how to ride a bicycle, but that will not enable you to ride a bicycle. You can read a manual about how to swim, but that won't enable you to jump in the water and start swimming. To intellectualize about sex is one thing. But it is not the same thing as the real thing. Babies do not learn how to eat by being told. They learn to eat by doing it. There may be books about how to be a basketball superstar or a concert pianist. But reading them won't get you there. You have to learn your moves and your eye-hand coordination by doing it – by practicing. Young children learn how to talk by imitating those around them. They can't even read a textbook that would tell them how. You can buy books about how to play chess, but you won't know how until you do it. You can read books about any subject. But their value is limited to talking to yourself or to others about what they "say." What you can know is unrelated to what you can actually do in any real world. Just because someone told you "how," you cannot drive a nail with a hammer without learning by doing. Knowing the physics of the process may have some currency with other physicists, but it does not enable you to drive the nail with a hammer without hitting your finger. You can, indeed, understand the process of seduction *intellectually*. But that doesn't enable you to be seductive. That requires learning how by doing.

Again, archiving in your mind some information about this or that may lead you to believe that what you know enables you to *do*. It doesn't. We are essentially made of habits – habits of thought, habits of feeling, habits of doing this or that in a way consistent with those habits, but not necessarily consistent with what may be called for. Willpower is not very effective with long ingrained habits. "You can be anything you want to be" many have been known to tell their offspring. This is a patently false assertion. People can only be what they are capable of being. If they have certain kinds of habits, they could possible become where those particular habits lead. If they have the wrong kinds of habits, it is very unlikely that they could be what they "want to" be.

This is a very pragmatic (because empirical) perspective. So it would take a pragmatic idealist to address that dilemma in a pragmatic way. That person was William James, sometimes referred to as the father of American psychology. He may have been that "father." But his perspective was not much adopted by psychologists – or by people in general. What James set forth in his writings is that you can't change yourself no matter how much you theorize about doing so, and no matter how much willpower you applied. You can only change yourself by performing not who you *are*, but by performing convincingly who you *intend to be*.

You change yourself by performing who you would be, not by accumulating knowledge about it. It is your habits that need to be changed. And the only way to do that is by *performing* the qualities you want to have. A self-help book is not of much help unless you perform who you want to be in your daily life. Habits are changeable only by dispelling them with the habits that will get you where you want to be – to become who you would be. Epictetus's (or James's) advice is easy to understand. But it is difficult to effect, since the only way of becoming who you want to be is by doing what you have to do – performing yourself *as if* you were already there.

We are each the main character in the story of our lives. It is how well we play that role that determines the outcome of the story. It is first a matter of choosing how the story needs to be told. Then it is a matter of imagining the plot, themes, and characters needed to make your story turn out the way you envision. It is who you need to be that matters, not what your past has been. If you are trying to accomplish something, you need to be in the thrall of that something, not your past.

It is how we *perform* our lives today and tomorrow that matters for our future, not who we think we "are" because we have always been that way.

+++++

We do not see the world as it is. We see our worlds according to who we are – that is, in and through our own personal perspectives on the people and the things and the events of our worlds, whatever they are and wherever they came from. So Shakespeare's perspective on the human condition is especially fruitful for how we have to perform our lives:

> *"All the world's a stage,*
> *And all the men and women merely players:*
> *They have their exits and their entrances;*
> *And one [person] in his time plays many parts...."*

Even though Shakespeare's is more often quoted, there were many similar observations both before and after his time. For example, Thomas Heywood wrote: *"The world's a theater, the earth a stage...."* The overall story is the one being written by the billions of people who preceded you, and the billions of people who are your contemporaries, and the billions of people who are their social progeny. They are making it up as they go along. Through their actions and interactions, through their talk and their doing, that story has a multitude of authors. We enter that story at birth and exit it at death. In between we will play many roles, both chosen and accidental.

The more immediate story in which we will play our roles is that of our own peculiar civilization, our own culture. That story has had millions of authors and the burden comes to us as our genetic and cultural history.

Then there is the story that imposes itself on us from the people we know and the choices we make. As much as we like to think that we make our own lives, we don't. The context in which we have our lives is one of interdependency – interdependent with the lives of those we know directly or indirectly, and with the things and the events of our time on earth. We don't emerge fully formed. Actually, given the interdependencies of our lives with other lives and what gets created therein, we are a work in progress from birth to death. The best we can do is make a life within these convoluted contexts. We never have a blank slate on which to create the story of our own experienced lives.

Finally there is the immediate scenarios you get involved in many times a day. If your purposes and intentions for getting into them are efficacious (that is, beneficent for everyone involved or influenced), your story has the best chance for turning out the way you want it to. In our world, you are both the influencer and the influenced. Those are roles you can neither abdicate nor delegate.

+++++

The best we can do looks something like this:

- The worthier the roles we choose or fall into, and the more ably we play them for the benefit of others, past and future, the better our own lives could be.

- The worthier and the more efficacious our personal causes and purposes in life, and the more effectively we fulfill them, the better our own lives could be.

It's how we *perform* life that matters, not what we happen to *know* from others or our own "experiences." This is James's principle of *"As-if."* If you perform your life as-if it were dedicated to the good of the larger whole, you will paradoxically have the best chance of being who you would be in the world you wish you lived in. It all depends upon your perspectives on your world.

+++++

A Brief on Adaptation

An essential perspective in all of this is the recognition that people are almost infinitely adaptable. Eskimos adapt to the bitter cold. Amazonian tribes adapt to the heat and humidity. Astronauts adapt to their weightlessness in space, deep sea divers to the conditions they encounter there. Babies adapt to their circumstances. Warriors adapt to theirs. Illiterate people adapt to their circumstances, literate people adapt to their circumstances. We adapt to the conditions over which we have no control. Otherwise, we figure out a way to control the conditions to suit us. What we might be able to control, we'll try to do so. What we can't control, we can usually adapt to.

Most people adapt to the social and physical environments they happen to be brought up in. They may dream of a different (even "better") life (as in *Dreaming of Cockaigne*). There has to be a better life than that of a peasant, a stand-up comedian, or a garbage collector.

But many if not most people shun the kinds of perspectives that might lead to a better life simply because it seems easier to them just to remain adapted to the conditions they have adapted to.

That may mean, in some instances, that the status quo – no matter how bad it might seem to the person – is often the choice. People don't change (or adapt) when they want to. They change or adapt when they have to. Some people wouldn't change their ways no matter how others might consider the change to be what they need. They don't see it that way. Being adapted to the way things are is the most common perspective there is. People may *know* they need to change for a better life. But they don't *do* it. What people are "used to" can be far more potent than what they say they "want" in life. And that's often the difference between knowing and doing....

"It is impossible to cheat life; there are no answers to the problems of life in the back of the book."

--Kierkegaard

Perspective 16

An Afterword

We see ourselves and our worlds in and through our perspectives on such things. Modified over time by ignorance and intention, those perspectives have three sources: (1) they are handed down to us in some variation by our immediate and ancient predecessors; (2) they are imposed upon us by the popular culture of our time and by our friends and influencers; and/or (3) we make them up on the spot to fit with our current and often idiosyncratic predilections about ourselves and our worlds. They are not tangible. We can only infer them from the way a person talks or behaves. They are tacit. They are the usually unarticulated parameters of our unique minds. They are the gatekeepers between our minds and our selves, and between us and the rest of the world that we interact with or talk about. Our perspectives guide us with respect to what we pay attention to, and how we do so. And as has long been observed by the great thinkers of history, what we pay attention to predicts to who we are and to who we will become. Ortega Y Gasset put it this way:

> *"Tell me to what you pay attention and I will tell you who you are."*

In other words, we become who we are as a result of what we pay attention to. And what we pay attention to is a matter of our perspectives on things. If you believe yourself to be more important than others or than what is going on in your world, you will devote more attention to what is going on within you than with what is going on in the rest of your world. In the world we share, young people may pay more attention to their "selfies" than they do to their homework. People in general may pay more attention to the television they consume than to their neighbors or friends. Gossip may get your attention, sources of wisdom may not.

Some perspectives may become dominant, thus subordinating dozens of other perspectives. Radical ideologies can become dominant for certain people. Other people may prefer perspectives that better suit their comfort zones. What you are curious about may capture your attention, whereas what is most familiar to you can lose its place in the hierarchy of perspectives that constitute who you are. When you fall in love, that new perspective may sideline many others. But when something ardently sought after is gained, it may lose its hold on your attention. Getting more money may be a dominant perspective for those climbing the ladder. But those who have lots of money do not have the same perspective as those who lust for more of it. When you're starving, you may not be able to think about much else than food. When you're sated, that perspective recedes.

So not only are our private perspectives self-organizing by a logic beyond our comprehension (or concern), but they come and go as the circumstances of our lives come and go. Some perspectives that made us what we are emerge early in life and may continue their influence throughout our lives. Others – particularly if we leave behind those people who were instrumental in creating them for us and their influence – we take on new perspectives. They will never be identical, but we will share similar perspectives with the people we most often hang out with directly or indirectly (those we don't know but whose work, like books or music lyrics, we pay attention to). If an experience we have affects us deeply, we may come out of that experience with a different perspective on ourselves or our worlds.

Most people don't choose their perspectives on things. They just sort of happen to us, adventitiously. We don't know specifically where they came from. Nor are we curious most of the time where they are leading us. Most people are not aware that they are being pulled and pushed here and there by their perspective on things, or on themselves. People don't generally know *why* they pay attention to what they pay attention to. Nor do they seem to care, even though their perspective on things will, as Ortega says, be the operant source of who they are and who they become. If you thought you were going to die, but don't, it is likely you will have a different perspective on your life. If your spouse, whom you expected to be with for the duration, dumps you for any reason, it is likely that you will thereby have a different perspective on the rest of your life...at least for a while.

If your life or your lifestyle change in some significant and basic way, your perspective on life and your world will change accordingly. If, on the other hand, your perspectives on life change in some significant way for any reason, your life and your lifestyle will be channeled by those different perspectives. Everyone you meet and with whom you have a relationship – especially if you move to a foreign land – will bring about changed perspectives on yourself and your world. Given that "the news" is these days global, you may have a perspective on the geopolitics of the world. Since there is little or nothing you can do about any such situation, the only value in that perspective is that you can talk to other people like you who are wasting their time, just needing some current event to talk about currently with like-minded people who prefer their perspective from the bleachers, not on any playing field. Certainly the perspective of the people who report the news is not the same as the perspective of the people who consume the news. You don't become newsworthy yourself unless you do something aberrant, or until you are the victim (or the perpetrator) of a big accident or terrorist attack. For the people who report the news, it is a way of making a living. For the people who consume the news, it may be no more than an addiction, which costs time but has no more than a mutual chin-wag for payoff.

+++++

It perhaps became apparent that the term *perspective* is in the vernacular somewhat like "point of view." There are two aspects of point of view that can serve you well. **One** is the recognition that your point of view, even if you are trying to see something from some other point of view, is yours alone. Whether you are reading or listening, it is your point of view that leads to your interpretation. Whether you are talking or writing, it is your listener's or your reader's point of view that leads them to their interpretation. People may have similar perspectives on the "same" event or thing. But their interpretations will be a function of *their* perspectives. We never see the world as *it* is. We see our worlds as *we* are.

The other has something to do with the intellectual sophistication of a particular person to take the point of view intended, for example, by a writer or an artist or a speaker. Novels are written from some point of view – for example, from one of the character's point of view, the protagonist's point of view, or the omniscient point of view provided by the author. Do you look at a painting from your point of view, the artist's point of view, or some expert's point of view? If you go to a performance by a stand-up comic, you go expecting to laugh. If you tune in to a performance by a politician, you will have a different point of view depending upon whether you are a conservative or a liberal. If you are a pupil, you will have a different point of view from the bureaucrat who wrote the curriculum. If you are a lover and want to remain so, you will take whatever point of view moves things along.

Even if you try to de-center yourself by trying to adapt to the other person's point of view, your way of doing so will come from you. There are individual points of view, and collective points of view. If you live and work in America, you will have a different point of view on things than will, say, the average Russian or the average Malaysian. Your point of view (your perspective) will be more American than will theirs. Whether yours or theirs, certain differing cultural (and sub-cultural) differences are a part of what people "are," and will therefore not be conscious to those people unless something happens to make that awareness necessary.

In his *Young Man Luther*, Erik Erikson coined the term "identity crisis." He was referring to how necessary it was for young people to forge a course for life utilizing some central perspective – and how seemingly it was for them to connect their pasts with their thoughts about their future. Actually, this kind of crisis can occur at any age. There is the mid-life crisis, for example, when people may realize how irrelevant their lives have been and will continue to be, unless they make some significant changes. Most will not make those changes, of course. They are more likely to settle for what they have, to adapt to the less-than-satisfactory conditions of their existence. An opportunity for pursuing an extracurricular affair may offer a temporary palliative for their "crisis." But in general, it is when their perspective on themselves gets out of whack with the perspective they assume others have on who they "are" that the identity crisis may occur. The struggle for whether a person determines his or her "identity" in the world, or the society determines his or her identity continues in varying degrees throughout our lifetimes.

One thing you can be certain of is that there will be a difference between how you see yourself and how you imagine others see you. When that difference gets to be too great for you, you then have some work to do about perspective, one way or the other. The other thing you can be certain of is that the richer (and thus the more propelling) the perspectives you can bring to bear on yourself and your world, the richer (and more compelling) your life will be.

In the "Author's Note" of her book *Them* (1969), Joyce Carol Oates offered an intriguing perspective:

> *"This is a work of history in fictional form – that is, in personal perspective, which is the only kind of history that exists."*

What she's suggesting is that everything occurs in personal perspective – in fictional form. You can *know* that. Or you can *do* that. *How* you make it a part of who you are and thus an impetus for your doing depends upon how you interpret it. We could all be a lot better at writing our histories. But that depends upon your perspective on your history.

"What each [person] does is based not on direct and certain knowledge, but on pictures made by himself or given to him....The way in which the world is imagined determines at any particular moment what [people] will do."

--Walter Lippmann, *Public Opinion*